T0399583

Death and Funeral Practices in Portugal

Academic studies on death and cemeteries are relatively recent in Portugal; those that do exist tend to adopt an essentially historical and artistic point of view. Studies on the practicalities of managing the dead and their spaces are even more recent, and they do not yet form a cohesive body of work.

Combining both approaches, *Death and Funeral Practices in Portugal* is the first book to offer a broad look at the evolution and current status of Portuguese funerary practice. By exploring the country's historical development, examining the contemporary legal framework, and systematizing the way Portugal manages its cemeteries, crematoria, and other death spaces, this book aims to provide an essential reference to researchers with an interest in Portuguese funeral practice. Among other themes, this book interprets the predominance of Catholic funerals, examines the relatively recent history of cremation, and contextualizes the practices of exhumation and grave re-use, which are integral to the normal functioning of a Portuguese cemetery.

This is the first book on Portuguese death and dying written specifically for a non-Portuguese audience. It will be of interest to researchers and scholars but also accessible to students and non-specialist readers first coming into the subject.

Rafaela Ferraz Ferreira is a writer and independent researcher with a focus on Portuguese death practices, specifically current and emerging forms of body disposal.

Ana Júlia Almeida Miranda works in Aveiro as a technical assistant of two public cemeteries, Esgueira and Taboeira, dealing with all the legal and bureaucratical matters of managing and maintaining the two cemeteries.

Francisco Queiroz is a Portuguese art historian, and researcher at both CEPESE (Oporto) and ARTIS-IHA/FLUL (Lisbon).

Routledge International Focus on Death and Funeral Practices

Series Editor – Julie Rugg, University of York, UK

Death Studies is an international and interdisciplinary endeavour and encompasses an interest in all mortality-related themes. This series of shortform books provides essential information on death and funeral practices in countries throughout the world.

Creating a common framework for understanding funeral rituals rests on definition and the description of processes, events and rituals which ostensibly appear the same but in actuality are markedly different, country to country. Each book has the same basic structure, which incorporates:

- historic, contextual background to understand how funeral practices have developed;
- burial and cremation rates, and change over time;
- an outline of key legislation guiding death registration, the funeral industry and cemetery and crematorium provision;
- what happens in the event of a death;
- an overview of the funeral industry including the ways in which funeral directing services are delivered and the balance of state/private involvement in funeral directing business;
- the cost of funerals and how they are paid for;
- church involvement in funerals and arrangements made for minority religious groups;
- a full and detailed description of a typical funeral;
- the provision of cemetery and crematorium services;
- patterns of commemoration

Fully referenced, and supported by relevant images, figures and tables, books in the series provide an essential research resource on practices, the law, and funeral-related procedures around the world. Collectively, the series provides an invaluable framework for international comparison.

This series is a continuation of *Funerary International*, a series distributed by Emerald Publishing. Four books were published in this legacy series: *Funerary Practices in England and Wales* (Rugg

& Parsons, 2018); *Funerary Practices in the Netherlands* (Mathijssen & Venhorst, 2019), *Funerary Practices in the Czech Republic* (Nešporová, 2021); and *Funerary Practices in Serbia* (Pavićević, 2021).

Death and Funeral Practices in Russia
Sergei Mokhov

Death and Funeral Practices in Portugal
Rafaela Ferraz Ferreira, Ana Júlia Almeida Miranda and Francisco Queiroz

For more information on the series please visit: www.routledge.com/Routledge-International-Focus-on-Death-and-Funeral-Practices/book-series/DEATH

Death and Funeral Practices in Portugal

Rafaela Ferraz Ferreira, Ana Júlia Almeida Miranda and Francisco Queiroz

Routledge
Taylor & Francis Group

LONDON AND NEW YORK

First published 2022
by Routledge
4 Park Square, Milton Park, Abingdon, Oxon OX14 4RN

and by Routledge
605 Third Avenue, New York, NY 10158

Routledge is an imprint of the Taylor & Francis Group, an informa business

British Library Cataloguing-in-Publication Data
A catalogue record for this book is available from the British Library

Library of Congress Cataloging-in-Publication Data
A catalog record has been requested for this book

ISBN: 978-0-367-72155-8 (hbk)
ISBN: 978-0-367-72157-2 (pbk)
ISBN: 978-1-003-15368-9 (ebk)

DOI: 10.4324/9781003153689

Typeset in Times New Roman
by codeMantra

Contents

Figures

Tables

Acknowledgments

The authors would like to thank several people for their contributions to this work: José Carlos Cidade Oliveira and Belmira Coutinho, researchers; Fernando Oliveira, funeral director at the Gamelas funeral home in Esgueira; António Matos, funeral director at the Fernão Magalhães funeral home in Oporto; Miguel Moreira, former manager of trade association AAFP and current owner of funerary company Funer OP; Sheikh David Munir of the Central Mosque of Lisbon; Rabbi Daniel Litvak of the Kadoorie Synagogue in Oporto. The authors apologize in advance for any omissions in this list.

We extend our gratitude to the cemeteries photographed in this book—particularly, the municipal cemeteries of Lisbon and Oporto, the local cemetery of Esgueira, and the private Lapa cemetery—for the goodwill that extends far beyond the scope of this volume.

Last, but not least, we would like to thank Julie Rugg for the kind invitation to represent Portugal in this international series.

1 Introduction

Portugal, officially the Portuguese Republic, is a sovereign state located in southwestern Europe, specifically the Iberian Peninsula. As the westernmost country in Europe, Portugal borders Spain on the north and east, and the Atlantic Ocean on the west and south. Its territory includes the autonomous regions of the Azores and Madeira, both of which have their own regional governments.

With a foundation date of 1143, Portugal is one of the oldest nation states in Europe, with borders that have remained virtually unchanged since the 13th century. This stability has resulted in what is, by all standards, a quite homogeneous nation. Portuguese is the official language, and it is spoken in all parts of the national territory. Roman Catholicism is the dominant religion. Although there are regional differences, which manifest in both cultural practice and socioeconomic status, there is a strong sense of Portuguese identity that prevails. There are no separatist movements in Portugal. Portugal is also considered to be one of the safest and most peaceful countries in the world—the third, in fact, according to the most recent Global Peace Index (Institute for Economics & Peace, 2020).

Portugal may enjoy great safety and political stability today, along with a strong democracy and freedom of press (EIU – Economist Intelligence Unit, 2021; RSF – Reporters Without Borders, 2020), but this has not always been the case. It was only in 1974 that the country escaped the longest-lasting authoritarian regime in 20th-century Europe, António de Oliveira Salazar's *Estado Novo*. The regime ended after 48 years, on the morning of April 25, 1974, with a bloodless coup known as the Carnation Revolution. With the end of the regime came, also, the end of the Portuguese Colonial War, which had been ongoing since the 1960s in Angola, Guinea-Bissau, and Mozambique, territories the Portuguese had colonized and now refused to give up.

DOI: 10.4324/9781003153689-1

The Estado Novo was just the last of a series of tumultuous regime changes in 19th- and 20th-century Portugal, which had direct impact on the evolution of funeral practices, as we explore in-depth in Chapter 2. In fact, the Estado Novo was born in 1933 out of the failure of a constitutional republic started in 1910 (referred to as the First Republic), which in turn resulted from a constitutional monarchy started in 1834. Prior to that, and since its foundation as a Christian Kingdom, Portugal had been an absolute monarchy, propped up by the Roman Catholic Church.

This speaks to the immense influence of the Roman Catholic Church over all aspects of Portuguese identity. Throughout Portuguese history, religion has enjoyed more stability than politics, and Portugal remains a markedly Catholic country to this day. Despite the fact that Portugal no longer professes an official religion, this has had little impact on cultural practice. Today, many Portuguese consider themselves to be non-practicing Catholics, and they regularly return to the Church for events such as weddings and, of course, funerals, as explored in Chapter 5.

There may be room for change with recent waves of immigration to the country. Traditionally, Portugal has been a country of emigrants: first to Africa and America, and then inside Europe. In recent years, however, many foreign communities have passed through or made a home in Portugal. The tumultuous decolonization process has brought immigrants from Angola and Mozambique, some of whom are Hindu and Muslim. Communities from Eastern Europe and China are now also significant, as well as communities from Britain and Central Europe, who mainly choose the country as a retirement destination. Apart from this latter group, who is concentrated in the south (and particularly in Algarve), foreign communities have mostly gathered in the cities of Lisbon and Oporto.

Demographically, Portugal exhibits a marked territorial imbalance; traditionally, urbanization has developed along the coast, resulting in a highly centralized country. At the 2011 census, Portugal had a population of 10.5 million people, a significant number of which lived in the metropolitan areas of Lisbon (2.8 million) and Oporto (1.8 million), two seaside cities. Lisbon was the only city in the country with over 500,000 inhabitants. This centralization is an historical feature of the country and it pervades all sorts of decisions. In fact, it is clear in the development of funerary practices, with Lisbon and Oporto leading the charge in the construction of public cemeteries in the 19th century, and then again in the adoption of cremation in the 20th century.

From an administrative perspective, the Portuguese territory is currently divided into municipalities (*municípios* or *concelhos*, which are usually named after a town or city but do not necessarily overlap with its limits), and, at a local level, civil parishes (*freguesias*). The archipelagos of Azores and Madeira have their own regional governments, but even in these regions, the territory is divided into municipalities and civil parishes. Municipalities and civil parishes are the entities that manage public cemeteries; for this reason, many practical decisions related to funerary administration happen at this level of government.

The current Portuguese Constitution ensures the separation of powers among four bodies: the President of the Republic, the Government, the Assembly of the Republic, and the Courts of law. The Assembly of the Republic, composed of up to 230 deputies serving four-year terms of office, is the main legislative body, although the Government also has limited legislative powers. Funerary legislation is issued by these two legislative bodies. However, specific regulations on cemeteries are also issued by municipalities and civil parishes.

Portugal is a developed and industrialized country. It is a member of multiple international organizations, most importantly: the United Nations, the North Atlantic Treaty Organization (NATO), the European Union, and the Community of Portuguese Language Countries (CPLP). Additionally, Portugal and the United Kingdom share the Anglo-Portuguese Alliance (Treaty of Windsor), the oldest alliance still in force today, which was signed in 1373. It is also a welfare state, providing universal health care, public education, social housing, and various other social services, including funerals.

References

EIU - Economist Intelligence Unit. (2021). *Democracy Index 2020: In Sickness and in Health?*

Institute for Economics & Peace. (2020). *Global Peace Index 2020: Measuring Peace in a Complex World.* http://visionofhumanity.org/reports

RSF - Reporters without Borders. (2020). *2020 World Press Freedom Index.* https://rsf.org/en/ranking/2020

2 History of Portuguese funerary practice

The 19th century

Portugal's first national cemetery laws were issued in the 1830s. Periods of high mortality, often associated with armed conflicts, had motivated the creation of a few local burial laws in the past, but never on a nationwide scale. The 1830s became, therefore, the official starting point in the history of the modern Portuguese cemetery.

Prior to that, the majority of burials took place inside the churches, or outside them in the *adro*. In Portugal, the word *adro* refers to an area around the church that served multiple communal purposes, from marketplace to burial ground. The concept is similar to that of the English 'churchyard,' but it differs from it in that the *adro* was not necessarily enclosed back then. It was a fully multifunctional space that flowed into the public square, and, for this reason, tombstones were not allowed on it—as they would get in the way of other uses for the space. Over the course of the 19th century, however, many *adros* came to be walled in: partially because marketplaces were moved to the outskirts, which allowed the Church to claim the *adro* for their own use, and partially because quite a few in rural areas were adapted into modern 'cemeteries' and were, therefore, walled in.

Up until the 1830s, burials were arranged and conducted by clergy or by religious associations of laypeople, such as Confrarias (*Confraternities*), Irmandades (*Brotherhoods*), or Ordens Terceiras (*Third Orders*). These associations (henceforth referred to as 'brotherhoods') had appeared in the Middle Ages and, befitting their semi-laic and semi-religious status, provided practical as well as spiritual assistance to their members in times of need, including at the time of death. It was not uncommon for a person to be a member of more than one brotherhood. Beyond arranging the funeral march and ensuring that the body was buried properly, in a sacred place such as inside the church

DOI: 10.4324/9781003153689-2

or in the *adro*, brotherhoods also arranged and celebrated masses for the souls of the deceased. These brotherhoods can be considered precursors to the funeral business. However, we are not aware of any work that outlines the history of the funeral industry in Portugal, so we cannot say how the shift develops, from these associations to the funeral industry as we know it today.

Burial in churches and *adros* tended to be socially stratified. The wealthier members of the community would be buried inside the church and close to the altars, in underground vaults closed with

Figure 2.1 The main square of Moreira de Rei, taken from the base of the pillory during an archaeological survey.

Note: The square, polarized by the medieval parish church, was the core of the village: where people met daily (before and after religious services), where local market was held, where notaries would write down contracts (possibly under a long-gone church wooden porch), where public announcements were made and criminals punished. And aside from all these functions, this was also the regular burial place for almost all the deceased in the village (others were buried inside the church). The border between the *adro* of the church and the square is, therefore, unclear. In a way, the *adro* is the religious extension of the square, and the square is the civic extension of the *adro*. Here, as in countless other Portuguese villages, the available space around the parish church was regularly used for burials from the Middle Age until the mid-19th century.

slabs bearing inscriptions and, when appropriate, even coats of arms. The rest of the community would occupy the remaining space, in communal or individual graves. If burial space ran out inside the church, then the *adro* would be used. More desirable parts of the *adro*, such as against the apse wall or before the front door, would sometimes be used even if there was enough space inside (Queiroz, 2002).

Portugal was not an isolated case: for centuries, church burial had been the norm in European Catholic countries. The practice began to garner criticism, in Portugal and elsewhere, in the 18th century, as the Age of Enlightenment created a new understanding of death and mortality. Scientific knowledge became more widespread in urban areas and concerns about public health moved to the forefront. The idea that decomposing bodies released noxious miasmas which could cause disease was popular among some authors of the late 18th and early 19th century. This idea led to the conviction that contact between the living and the dead should be avoided, and that bodies should be buried at reasonable distance from the community—not so far that they were exiled from it, but not so close that their miasmas could cause disease. For the sake of public health, state authorities were called to intervene in the realm of the dead, which up until then had been solely the domain of the Catholic Church.

Early attempts at regulating burial and cemeteries, issued occasionally through the first three decades of the 19th century, produced little results, and the traditional practice of church burial remained the norm. The exception was the hospital burial grounds. These were not really cemeteries, because in those days hospitals were mostly used by migrants, pilgrims, military (in case of armed conflict), and above all, very poor people who could not afford to call a doctor or pay the pharmacy bill. Thus, the majority of the burial grounds of hospitals had only walls, a door, and several temporary graves, with no monuments whatsoever. However, some were embellished to gain more dignity, as it happened in Viana do Castelo or in Setúbal (Queiroz & Portela, 2003).

The cholera epidemic that hit Portuguese ports in 1833, spreading out to other regions and causing a high death toll in the country, brought new urgency to the matter. The ongoing civil war, by then in its second year, only added to the death toll. On June 18, 1833, the government issued a *Portaria* that forbade burials inside the churches and cloisters of the largest Portuguese city: Lisbon. To replace these traditional burial places, the government established public burial grounds at Prazeres and Alto de São João in the outskirts of the city.

Figure 2.2 Tile panel representing a typical burial in the 1770s in Setúbal.

Note: It represents a typical burial in the 1770s of a deceased in a hospital run by a brotherhood. The deceased died in the hospital probably because they had no family or were very poor.

These would, later, become the first municipal cemeteries in Lisbon (Queiroz, 2002).

A decree issued on September 21, 1835, one year after the end of the civil war, expanded on the *Portaria* of 1833, with the intent of extending the prohibition of church burial to the entire country. New public cemeteries should be built to replace both traditional burial places and temporary burial grounds used during the war. The underlying assumption was that, if the cholera epidemic and the civil war had shifted the dead away from the church floor, it made sense to issue further legislation to bury them in an orderly manner elsewhere: in the new public cemetery (Queiroz & Rugg, 2003).

No longer relying solely on public health arguments, the 1835 decree was also grounded in concepts like individualism and memorialization, modernity and urbanity, civilization and citizenship. It tried to place funerary practice and cemetery administration in the hands of secular authorities, effectively taking over from the Catholic Church. In order to do this without immediate backlash, in the form of mass protests instigated by religious authorities, the decree

Figure 2.3 People kneeling over graves while attending a religious service at the church of São Nicolau in Oporto (lithography based on a drawing of Joseph James Forrester, 1835).

Source: Forrester, J. J., Lane, R. J., & Childs, G. (1835). Igreja de S. Nicholao, Porto – Church of St. Nicholas, Oporto [Lithography]. National Library of Portugal. https://purl.pt/6130.

appealed to the religious sentiment of the Portuguese population. It described the traditional practice of church burial as superstitious and even offensive, referring back to the Catholic bans on church burial made in Papal Councils in the Middle Ages (Queiroz, 2002).

The theological argument demonstrated a willingness to work with the Catholic Church in the construction of a new funerary paradigm. This collaboration, however, would be strained, as the Church had more to lose than simply spiritual authority: for instance, the revenue derived from burial fees, which up until then had reverted to the religious parishes and brotherhoods that administered burial grounds, would now revert to local government.

The 1835 decree can be summarized as follows:

- There should be a public cemetery in every town and village, established at least 143 meters from residential areas and enclosed by a wall with a minimum height of 225 cm;
- The cemetery should be large enough to accommodate five times the yearly average of local deaths;
- Bodies should be buried in individual graves with a minimum depth of 125 cm;
- Although public, the entire area of the cemetery should be consecrated before any burials could take place. If a priest permitted burial outside the public cemetery, he would be deprived of his earnings (Queiroz, 2002).

The 1835 decree proved innovative on two accounts. First, it separated the cemetery from the church (physically, if not spiritually) and moved it to the outskirts of the community. Second, it specifically called for burial in individual graves while allowing for ornamentation and memorialization. Whereas the construction of tombstones had been discouraged or downright forbidden in the *adro* due to its multifunctional character, the public cemetery would present no such difficulty.

Public resistance to the enactment of the innovative 1835 decree was very strong, especially outside Lisbon and Oporto—by then the only large cities in the country, with over 50,000 inhabitants (Queiroz & Rugg, 2003). Protests were common through the following decades, and many fed on unresolved social tensions left behind by the civil war, as the public cemetery was perceived as a hallmark of the new liberal regime. One of these protests against public cemeteries, in 1846, was even at the root of several riots which brought the country almost to another civil war protest in Portugal. This crisis became known as Maria da Fonte, after the nickname given to the woman who allegedly led the group of peasants that forced a burial inside the local church, against all regulations.

Here are a few examples of measures taken to address the public resistance. Oporto, for instance, suffered a lot from the aforementioned civil war, being besieged for many months. The city's *intelligentsia*, mainly made up of former exiles in the most cosmopolitan cities in Europe, recognized the need for a public burial ground. However, Catholic brotherhoods held a hegemony over funeral business in the city, administering their own private burial grounds inside or around their churches. Foreseeing the compulsory construction of at least one public cemetery in Oporto, these brotherhoods soon decided to improve their cemeteries in order to be able to keep them open, invoking previous ordinances that had authorized their existence. One particular brotherhood, the Lapa brotherhood, thanks to the vision of the businessman João da Silva Ribeiro, invested so heavily in improving its burial space that it even decided to rebuild it in the open air, with a beautiful entrance portal. Although this new cemetery was close to the Lapa church, it complied with all the main norms of the 1835 law, except for the fact that it was not a public cemetery, but a private one. Nevertheless, it became tolerated by local authorities. In fact, several members of local government belonged to the Lapa brotherhood, and they would prefer to have their final resting places in the newly embellished private cemetery, rather than in the planned public cemetery. Thus, contrary to what happened in Lisbon, in Oporto the most important cemetery to be built following the 1835 law was not a public one. Oporto would only have its first municipal and public cemetery, at Prado do Repouso, some years after the liberal faction had won the war, in 1839 (Queiroz, 2002). However, large areas of this cemetery were kept as a farm for many years, and during this period, the municipality received more revenues from its pastures than from graves. During the 1840s and the 1850s, Prado do Repouso was the unofficial cemetery for the poorer in Oporto. A second public cemetery, at Agramonte, would open only in 1855, partly due to a second cholera epidemic. Agramonte was founded in a rather careless way. Thus, it replaced Prado do Repouso as the public cemetery of Oporto for the poorer until the late 1860s. In fact, by then all the private cemeteries belonging to brotherhoods that were entangled in the city core were closed down by local authorities. As a result, these brotherhoods demanded large private plots in Prado do Repouso and Agramonte to relocate their former cemeteries. This led to a rapid embellishment of the first and to a complete landscape redesign of the second.

Despite their more or less hesitant beginnings, all four of the public cemeteries mentioned up until this point—Prazeres and Alto de

Figure 2.4 Partial view of the older plots at the Lapa Cemetery in Oporto.

Note: The cemetery was officially founded in 1833, but major construction work started in 1836. The cemetery was only consecrated in 1838.

São João in Lisbon, Prado do Repouso and Agramonte in Oporto—are now considered historical. We explore the musealization of these spaces in Chapter 12.

In what concerns the construction of public cemeteries in villages, towns, and smaller cities, generally the Northern half of the country was more antagonistic and less proactive. A more fervent, deeply rooted approach to Catholicism, along with a scattered form of urbanization, where the parish church could be virtually isolated and surrounded only by land, combined to create a certain leniency toward the adoption of the new burial paradigm. Meanwhile, in the South, where settlements were densely packed, the parish church could be landlocked in a residential area, making burial in the church and *adro* less tolerable. Even so, some of the oldest public cemeteries in smaller cities, like Viana do Castelo, Aveiro, Figueira da Foz, and Santarém or Évora, among others, were actually established within former monasteries, which had been appropriated by the State after the dissolution of religious orders in 1834. There were several reasons for this occupation of former monasteries: the area was already walled in, it was close enough to a sacred place, and there was enough infrastructure to adapt into facilities for the new public cemetery. In many cases, the enclosures had already served as ad hoc burial grounds during the cholera epidemic of 1833, so local administrations found it more suitable to use them (Queiroz, 2016). This solution was considerably cheaper than to build a cemetery from scratch in the outskirts, which sometimes even demanded a new road. Thus, even if this approach was not sufficient for cities such as Lisbon and Oporto, where cemeteries had to be significantly larger, it was the ideal solution in smaller cities and towns.

Where it was not possible to nationalize a monastery, or if the existing ones were not available (nuns were allowed to live in the nationalized monasteries until the last one had died), or if its location was not suitable, then a similar solution could be adopted: establishing the public cemetery in a former castle, like it happened in the towns of Montemor-o-Velho, Torres Novas, or Santiago do Cacém. In fact,

Figure 2.5 The public cemetery of Arcos de Valdevez.

Note: It was built next to a nationalized monastery, not in its enclosure but right in front of its church, which became the mortuary chapel.

almost all the castles belonged to the State and were surrounded by solid walls (even if somewhat ruined). Castles were also in high and well-ventilated spots, and sometimes even had a religious building nearby that could be adapted into a mortuary chapel.

Establishing public cemeteries in the land of old nationalized monasteries and in abandoned castles was a common solution in the years that followed the publication of the first public cemetery law of 1835 (Queiroz, 2002). This was a way to work around the unappealing quality of the first public cemeteries, which many municipalities had built with wooden walls and doors and with insufficient landscaping. These bare burial grounds were generally disliked by populations, and sometimes, only the poor with no relatives were buried in them. However, public cemeteries that were placed inside nationalized monasteries and abandoned castles with a church nearby tended to be more easily accepted. As a result, these cemeteries saw the construction of monuments in their early years, and they have endured to this day. Conversely, early public cemeteries of the late 1830s and the 1840s were so carelessly built and so much disapproved by the locals that they were replaced afterward, by other cemeteries in other locations (Queiroz, 2002).

Figure 2.6 The cemetery of Santiago do Cacém was built inside the medieval castle, which also encloses the parish church.

It was so difficult to establish proper and definitive public cemeteries in the rural areas of Portugal in the years after 1835 that, in 1844 a new law on this matter, reinforcing the former one, stated that at least there should be a municipal cemetery in every municipality—which means that there were still many Portuguese municipalities without a cemetery built in accordance with the 1835 law. Burials continued to take place in the *adros*, and sometimes even inside the churches, despite being forbidden since 1835.

By the mid-1870s, almost all the municipalities in Portugal had, finally, at least one public cemetery—even if the new sites did not always respect requirements regarding the distance from residential areas, and were built just meters from the local church (Queiroz & Rugg, 2003). Likewise, mass graves remained in use in the largest Lisbon cemeteries until the late 19th century, despite the call for more individualized burial. Between 1874 and 1878, 30.1% and 60.4% of all bodies buried at Prazeres and Alto de São João cemeteries, respectively, were placed in mass graves (Catroga, 1991). This statistic also reveals us that Prazeres was substantially more elite than Alto de São João, where the percentage of poorer people buried was larger.

In the 1890s, there were still several villages whose public cemetery was yet to be built, even in areas within 20 km of Lisbon and Oporto (Queiroz, 1999). However, by those days, burials inside the churches were already very rare. In the villages where there was not a public cemetery yet, burials usually would take place in the *adro*.

The negative attitudes displayed by many communities toward public cemeteries during the second and the last third of the 19th century highlight the disconnect between lawmakers and the public in the matter of death practices. Legal changes inspired by the new scientific principles of public health were perceived as an attack on traditional religious practices (Catroga, 1999).

In the 1870s, new legislation made it mandatory for public cemeteries to include a separate unconsecrated section, with its own wall and direct access from the street, even in towns and villages where the entirety of the population was Catholic. The debate surrounding cremation, which developed while much of the country was still transitioning out of the practice of church burial, emerged in Portugal in the 1870s, inspired by the pro-cremation debates happening throughout Europe (Catroga, 1999; Queiroz, 2005). When the issue of expanding the public cemetery at Prazeres was discussed in 1876, the Marquis of Sousa Holstein proposed cremation as

Figure 2.7 Some graves in the *adro* that surrounds the parish church of Anha in the municipality of Viana do Castelo.

Note: This *adro* was enclosed and served as the local cemetery until a proper cemetery was built right next to it, behind the church.

an alternative solution to the problem of cemetery overcrowding (Queiroz, 2005), even though, in those days, such problem applied merely to a couple of cemeteries in the cities of Lisbon and Oporto. Likewise, doctors such as Bernardino Passos published dissertations on the subject of cremation, lending further credibility to the practice (Catroga, 1999; Passos, 1878). Although support for cremation was also motivated by secularist beliefs, these were mostly silenced during this period (Catroga, 1999); instead, cremation was presented as a clean, practical, hygienic alternative that would not only reduce maintenance costs associated with expanding public cemeteries, but also limit the spread of disease from dead bodies in public cemeteries.

Concerns regarding the impact of cemeteries on public health turned out to be unfounded. In 1885, researcher Ricardo Jorge analyzed air and water samples from the public cemeteries in Lisbon and Oporto and found them to be harmless. According to his conclusions, as long as public cemeteries were established on suitable soil and built in accordance with sanitary standards, they would not harm public health (Jorge, 1885). Although this study did not produce immediate effects, over time it helped overthrow the public health argument in support of cremation (Queiroz, 2005).

The 19th century also saw the officialization of the activity of coroners. The teaching of forensic medicine (referred to in Portugal as *medicina legal*, literally 'legal medicine') in Portugal began in the first half of the 19th century, at the University of Coimbra. However, it was only in 1899 that Portugal organized its first forensic medicine services, creating three morgues to function as annexes to the Faculties of Medicine in Coimbra, Lisbon, and Oporto. These morgues were created in order to guarantee that doctors could perform autopsies and offer practical training in forensic medicine. The concept of forensic medicine was, however, not limited to autopsies; it also included other types of scientific investigation in the fields of psychiatry and toxicology, for example.

The 20th century

The Republican Revolution of 1910 overthrew the constitutional monarchy and replaced it with the secular and actively anticlerical First Republic. The First Republic targeted the Catholic Church in multiple ways: many parish assets were nationalized, religious holidays were abolished, divorce was legalized, and practices associated with death and dying were promptly secularized. With the Constitution of the First Republic, published in 1911, public cemeteries became secular and available to all religions. Accordingly, the walls that, in some cemeteries, had previously separated the consecrated and non-consecrated sections were torn down. In the new secular Republic, no atheist could be made to feel segregated in a public place.

In line with its secularist ideals, the First Republic also issued the *Código de Registo Civil* (Code of Civil Registry) of February 18, 1911, a legal document that stated how individuals would henceforth be bound to the State rather than the Church. In practice, this meant that, for the first time in Portuguese history, the civil registry of births, marriages, and deaths would take primacy over parish records. Death registration as a civil act for all citizens began, therefore, in 1911. The Catholic Church continued to produce parish records, and it continues to do so today, but they no longer serve the purpose of primary register of the Portuguese population.

The *Código de Registo Civil* of 1911 also took the important step of legalizing cremation. Despite the fact that support for cremation was never widespread, the practice had become synonymous with a new, more secular funerary paradigm; as such, its legalization was firmly in line with the progressive spirit of the First Republic (Catroga, 1999). Nevertheless, burial remained the norm, with the *Código* itself stating, in article 265°, that requests for cremation all had to be individually approved based on the analysis of four distinct documents. Plans for the construction of the country's first crematorium—at Lisbon's Alto de São João Cemetery—began the next year, but the work was only completed in November 1925, 13 years later (Xisto, 2012). Only 22 cremations were conducted between 1925 and 1936 (Queiroz, 2005; Xisto, 2012).

In addition to the changes that occurred in the registration of deaths, secularization of cemeteries, and legalization of cremation, the period of the First Republic was also relevant because of two mortality crises that greatly affected the country: the First World War (often referred to as the Great War, as Portugal did not participate in the Second World War) and the Spanish influenza epidemic.

Portugal did not officially enter the war, on the side of the Allied Powers, until 1916. However, prior to that, Portuguese troops had already fought with German troops in Angola and Mozambique, which were occupied by Portugal at the time. Upon official entry into the war, Portuguese forces were deployed to the Western front through the newly created Portuguese Expeditionary Corps (commonly known as CEP, from '*Corpo Expedicionário Português*'). At the same time, troops continued to fight in Angola and Mozambique. The death toll of the First World War is estimated to have been between 7,100 and 8,300 soldiers; of these, around 2,000 will have died in France, 800 in Angola, and 4,800 in Mozambique. The *Memorial Virtual aos Mortos da Grande Guerra* (Virtual Memorial to the Dead of the Great War), an official online memorial created in 2014, identified at least 6.232 of these losses (Arquivo Histórico Militar, 2014; J. C. M. Tavares, 2019; J. M. Tavares, 2018).

Most of the war dead were buried abroad, but the handling of the dead differed from the European to the African war theaters. In France, the desire to gather the bodies of Portuguese soldiers manifested soon after the war ended, with the creation of the *Cimetière Militaire Portugais de Richebourg-l'Avoué* (Portuguese Military Cemetery of Richebourg-l'Avoué). Today, this cemetery houses the bodies of 1.831 soldiers previously buried in scattered cemeteries across Germany, Belgium, France, and the Netherlands (Tavares, 2018). In Angola and Mozambique, the war dead remain scattered.

Portugal never established military cemeteries on national territory; however, many public cemeteries have a dedicated military plot.

These private plots are called *Talhões de Combatentes*, or combatant's plots, and they are acquired and maintained by the *Liga dos Combatentes*, an association created in 1921 to bring together Portuguese soldiers from the First World War. *Talhões de Combatentes* house the graves of war dead as well as war veterans, and they are characterized by the uniformity of the grave monuments, which usually consist of a simple, obelisk-shaped headstone with minimal decoration beyond the emblem of the *Liga dos Combatentes*. Although, in Portugal, the *Liga dos Combatentes* is better known for maintaining these private plots, it has also been instrumental in the discovery and maintenance of war graves abroad.

Concurrently to the First World War, Portugal was also affected by the Spanish influenza epidemic of 1918—commonly referred to in Portugal as *gripe pneumónica*. The virus began to spread from the Spanish border in May 1918 (Sequeira, 2001), and it is estimated to have killed 135,257 people in 1918 and 1919. Lisbon and Oporto saw the greatest number of deaths: 18,338 and 17,865, respectively (Bandeira, 2009). Comparing the total number of deaths with a total population of around six million people,[1] we can estimate that the epidemic killed 2% of the Portuguese population.

Although public health concerns had become more prominent during the 19th century, as we have seen in the context of the creation of public cemeteries, state intervention in the matters of health and hygiene was still very deficient (Sobral & Lima, 2018). The epidemic placed public health entities under enormous pressure, which combined with a lack of doctors—many of whom had been mobilized to the war front (Sequeira, 2001)—could only spell disaster. Prophylactic measures imposed by the Directorate-General for Health (DGS) at the beginning of October 1918 were largely ineffective, and the influenza epidemic tore through Portuguese society.

In Lisbon, the problems around the management of the dead from the influenza epidemic are well-documented. City hall fought cemetery overcrowding by burying bodies in land adjacent to the cemeteries, purchasing land for extensions when possible, and ordering that the dead were buried outside their area of residence if their local cemetery was full. In order to avoid the accumulation of dead bodies in the hospital morgues, bodies that went unclaimed for 24 hours were wrapped in burlap and buried in a mass grave. It is estimated that over 600 people who had died in the city's hospitals were buried in mass graves (Relvas & Rijo, 2020). Society rallied to avoid this and provide individual burials when possible, with mutual aid associations becoming instrumental in that quest (Garnel, 2009). All in all, the influenza epidemic had a major demographic impact. According to the information contained in the report of the 1920 census, the mortality rate climbed to 40.18 in 1918, from values that had been around 20 in the three previous years (Direção Geral de Estatística da República Portuguesa, 1923). In spite of this, many authors agree that the epidemic was not recorded in collective memory with the same fervor as the First World War.

In 1926, a military coup put an end to the First Republic and inaugurated a dictatorship that would later develop into the *Estado Novo*, one of the longest-surviving authoritarian regimes in Europe, which lasted until 1974. The *Estado Novo* was a conservative, nationalistic, and overtly Catholic regime that held '*Deus, Pátria e Família*' (God, Motherland, and Family) as its motto. In terms of death practices, the *Estado Novo* did not concern itself with doing away with the previous funerary paradigm. Public cemeteries retained their secular quality, as confirmed in the Constitution of 1933. In 1962, the government issued Decree 44220 to update and simplify guidance for the construction of cemeteries. This document is analyzed in-depth in Chapter 9, as it remains in effect today and provides answers to many practical questions regarding the appearance and organization of Portuguese cemeteries.

All in all, the *Estado Novo* was a period of consolidation for the practice of burial in public cemeteries, and stagnation for the practice of cremation. Cremation remained legal, as confirmed in the *Código do Registo Civil* of 1932. However, it had no practical expression, as the only crematorium in the country, at Alto de São João Cemetery, was closed in 1936 (Queiroz, 2005; Xisto, 2012).

Between 1961 and 1974, Portugal was involved in another war, known as the Portuguese Colonial War, which took place in the occupied territories of Angola, Guinea-Bissau, and Mozambique. On the Portuguese side, the war was sustained by the *Estado Novo* belief that the colonial territories were an inalienable part of the national territory. Meanwhile, liberation movements in colonized territories defended their own right to independence. It is estimated that Portuguese troops experienced around 8,000 deaths throughout the course of the war (Centro de Documentação 25 de Abril, 2002). Recent sources estimate the number to be much higher, at around 10,000 (Sousa, 2021).

Estado Novo policy in the first years of the war stated that soldiers who were killed in combat should be buried in cemeteries organized by their military units on the ground. If families wished to repatriate the bodies, they had to support the costs themselves (Associação 25 de Abril, 2020). As the war advanced, the government began to provide free transport for the bodies of the war dead; however, it would not support any additional costs with funerals or burial (Santos, 2019). It is estimated that 3,700 bodies of Portuguese soldiers who fell in combat are still buried in the theaters of war in Angola, Mozambique, and Guinea-Bissau (Santos, 2019). Efforts to repatriate the bodies are still ongoing, and progress is often reported in the press. The *Liga dos Combatentes* is part of these efforts abroad; in Portugal, it continues to bury war dead and war veterans in dedicated *Talhões dos Combatentes*, just like it had done for the soldiers of the First World War. Originally created for the dead of the First World War, the *Talhões dos Combatentes* now harbor the dead from two different wars fought in the 20th century.

The Portuguese Colonial War ended on April 25, 1974, when a military coup in Lisbon put an end to the *Estado Novo* and reinstated democracy, inaugurating the Third Republic that lasts to this day. After the coup, Portugal released its colonies, which created a wave of immigration to the country; Hindu immigrants, in particular, would contribute to change in funeral practice by lobbying for the reactivation of the country's only crematorium, as discussed in Chapter 5.

In 1998, the publication of Decree-Law 411/98 modernized Portuguese funerary law by centralizing and establishing the main guidelines for the transportation and disposal of dead bodies, skeletal remains, and cremation ashes. Rather than being guided by hygienist or secularist motivations, like some of its predecessors, this legal document, which remains in use today, shows a greater concern for the daily and practical challenges of cemetery administration: it recognizes that shortage of burial space presents a serious problem to the entities in charge of administering cemeteries in areas of demographic expansion and, accordingly, puts forth a series of policies to help fix the problem. As such, DL 411/98 brings three important changes: it recognizes burial and cremation as equally valid practices, reduces the resting time for temporary graves and exhumation from five to three years, and introduces the legal concept of aerobic decomposition module, essentially a form of entombment that aims to speed up decomposition and, therefore, increase the rate of grave turnover.

The 21st century

The issue of cemetery overcrowding remained a concern into the 21st century. The construction of crematoria has accelerated, especially in urban areas around the cities of Lisbon and Oporto. By the end of 2020, there were 34 crematoria in Portuguese territory. Cremation rates have also been growing, and numbers reported in the press indicate a 18.78% cremation rate in 2019 (Salvador, 2020).

At the turn of the 21st century, there was a major change in the organization of coroner services in Portugal. In 2001, the three Forensic Medicine Institutes (which had been called morgues until 1918) in Lisbon, Oporto, and Coimbra were merged, through Decreto-Lei 96/2001, into a single National Institute of Forensic Medicine, with headquarters in Coimbra. In 2012, the National Institute of Forensic Medicine was officially renamed National Institute of Legal Medicine and Forensic Sciences (*Instituto Nacional de Medicina Legal e Ciências Forenses*) by Decreto-Lei 166/2012. In its current configuration, the National Institute of Legal Medicine and Forensic Sciences is a central body with jurisdiction over the entire national territory, which has *delegações* (delegations) in Oporto, Coimbra, and Lisbon, under which smaller medicolegal *gabinetes* (offices) operate. Far from harboring only the work of coroners, the Institute is home to *médicos legistas* (literally 'legal doctors') and multiple specialists who not only conduct scientific research and train doctors and jurists, but also assist crime victims through clinical guidance and risk assessment. The Portuguese concept of *médico legista* is wider than that of coroner, as a *médico legista* is a medical doctor who conducts medical exams both in vivo and postmortem.

In the 21st century, the Portuguese government published further funerary legislation, mostly focused on the funerary industry rather than cemetery administration. Funeral homes (*agências funerárias* in Portuguese) as we know them today existed before the publication of this new legislation. However, as we have already mentioned, we are not aware of any study that addresses the history of the funeral industry in Portugal, so we cannot say to what extent this law changed the industry on a practical level. What we can say, however, is that this legislation marks the modernization of the sector, especially considering its publication shortly after Decree-Law 411/98 which, as we have seen, came to modernize the Portuguese funeral law at large.

The first of the new laws on the funeral industry, Decree-Law 206/2001, has already been revoked, reflecting the speed with which the legislation in the funeral sector is suffering changes and updates. It was replaced by Decree-Law 109/2010 of October 14, which establishes the regime for access to and exercise of the funeral activity and remains in force today. Decree-Law 109/2010 defines funeral activity as the provision of services related to the organization and realization of funerals, or services related to the transportation, burial, exhumation, cremation, repatriation, and transfer of bodies or remains. In addition to these main activities, which make up the core of what is considered to be the funeral activity in Portugal, Decree-Law 109/2010 also lists complementary activities that can be practiced by funeral homes. One such activity, thanatopraxy (a form of temporary preservation of the body for viewing purposes), was later regulated in 2015, in *Portaria* 162-A/2015 of July 1.

Decree-Law 109/2010 also introduced a major change by allowing private entities to manage public cemeteries through public–private partnerships. Prior to this, the division between public and private responsibilities in the funeral sector had been clear: local public entities managed public cemeteries, but did not offer funeral services; meanwhile, private entities provided funeral services, but did not manage cemeteries. Catholic brotherhoods that retained the administration of their private 19th-century cemeteries were the exception. This legal document was, therefore, instrumental in expanding the reach of private entities in the funeral sector. We discuss this in greater depth in Chapter 3.

This shift in legislative focus, coupled with the arrival of multinational funeral corporations to an industry that, previously, had been made up of small family-owned funeral homes, created the conditions for greater professionalization in the funeral sector. With new legislation and new players in the field, there is potential for the funeral sector to grow into a competitive and fast-paced field, driven by innovation rather than tradition. Although it is too early to say where it will lead, the professionalization of the sector could be considered one of the biggest developments of the 21st century, so far.

It is too early to say, too, whether Portuguese society will continue to secularize, or whether the cultural and religious influence of Catholicism will continue to appear in times of death. Data from 2010 indicated that 80% to 90% of all funerals were Catholic ("Funerais Laicos Ainda São Uma Minoria," 2010), a high rate for a society where only 56.1% of Catholics consider themselves to be actively practicing their religion (Secretariado Nacional da Pastoral da Cultura, 2012).

Another development of the 21st century that may have an impact on funeral practices is the COVID-19 pandemic. The novel coronavirus was confirmed to have reached Portugal on March 2, 2020. Shortly after, the Directorate-General for Health (*Direção-Geral da Saúde*, abbreviated and most often referred to as DGS) issued a series of guidelines for the handling of bodies of deceased COVID patients (Direção-Geral da Saúde, 2020b). One of the recommendations with the most implications for funeral practice stated that the body should be placed inside a waterproof body bag, and then inside a coffin, which should remain closed through all funeral proceedings. The recommendation also stated that cremation should be preferred to burial; however, this was not mandatory. Shortly after, the National Association of Mortuary Companies (*Associação Nacional de Empresas Lutuosas*, or ANEL), the largest Portuguese organization of companies in the funeral sector, established in 1990, issued a specific set of recommendations to be followed at all funerals regardless of the cause of death. The recommendations added, importantly, that wakes should be avoided, and that funerals should proceed directly from the place of death to the cemetery or crematorium (Associação Nacional de Empresas Lutuosas, 2020). Beyond these recommendations, the country also experienced national measures relating to funerals: under the National State of Emergency, funerals were limited to a maximum number of people, to be determined by the management of each cemetery. For November 1, *Dia de Todos os Santos*, the day when the Portuguese usually visit the cemetery to tend to graves, there was a ban on circulation between municipalities, as it was considered that the great mobility of people on this day was high-risk.

By December 31, 2020, a total of 413,678 confirmed cases of COVID-19 and 6,906 deaths had been reported (Direção-Geral da Saúde, 2020a). It is too early to say whether the COVID-19 pandemic will have a lasting demographic impact. Likewise, we cannot say whether it will be a catalyst for change in the funeral sector. Thus far, the pandemic has already changed funeral practices in small ways, by leading authorities to disavow public wakes and recommend direct burial, or even cremation, instead. This is a significant adjustment from the way Portuguese families and communities traditionally experience loss, and there is no telling whether it will lead to long-term change.

The future

Overall, recent changes in funeral practice have arrived in Portugal as an import from other countries to which the country is exposed. Thanatopraxy, for example, is growing in popularity now in the 21st century, as other countries begin to move away from it and into greener death practices. In the last 300 years, foreign communities have played a part in the development of funeral practices: the first cemeteries that are still in use were established by Protestants, and there is evidence to suggest that the Hindu community was influential in the redevelopment of cremation in the late 20th century. Other changes are also occurring in tandem with shifts in consumer behavior: for example, there is already a desire for greener and more individualized funerals. In fact, the current situation in terms of funeral practices is one of rapid and continuous change, which makes it difficult to predict future directions in many of the themes that we will discuss in the following chapters.

Note

1 According to the 1911 census, Portugal had 5.96 million inhabitants (Direção Geral de Estatística da República Portuguesa, 1913). By the 1920 census, it had barely surpassed six million inhabitants. The 1920 report points out that the population had been expected to grow to 6.4 million inhabitants, but that the deficit could be attributed to two causes: the First World War and the influenza epidemic (Direção Geral de Estatística da República Portuguesa, 1923).

References

Arquivo Histórico Militar. (2014). *Memorial Virtual aos Mortos da Grande Guerra*. http://www.memorialvirtual.defesa.pt/Paginas/Splash.aspx

Associação 25 de Abril. (2020). *Mortos—Morte e dor*. https://guerracolonial. pt/site/feridas-de-guerra/feridas-de-guerra-mortos-feridos-e-prisioneiros/ mortos/

Associação Nacional de Empresas Lutuosas. (2020). *Comunicado à Imprensa—Covid-19/Coronavírus: Recomendações de Procedimentos para Funerais*. https://www.anel.pt/storage/docs/sTXNtpVXE0nc94HAT02cCFj hnWqiR8SAOCuYVExE.pdf

Bandeira, M. L. (2009). A sobremortalidade de 1918 em Portugal: Análise demográfica. In J. M. Sobrol *et al.* (eds.) *A Pandemia Esquecida: Olhares comparados sobre a pneumónica 1918–1919* (pp. 131–154). Imprensa de Ciências Sociais.

Catroga, F. (1991). Revolução e secularização dos cemitérios em Portugal (inumistas e cremacionistas). In A. M. Coelho (ed.) *Atitudes Perante a Morte* (pp. 95–176). Edições Minerva.

Catroga, F. (1999). *O céu da memória: Cemitério romântico e o culto cívico dos mortos*. Edições Minerva.

Centro de Documentação 25 de Abril. (2002). *Guerra Colonial—Efectivos*. http://www.cd25a.uc.pt/index.php?r=site/page&view=itempage &p=1669

Direção-Geral da Saúde. (2020a). *Covid-19—Relatório De Situação— 31-12-2020*. https://covid19.min-saude.pt/wp-content/uploads/2020/12/304_ DGS_boletim_20201231-002.pdf

Direção-Geral da Saúde. (2020b). *Norma da Direção-Geral da Saúde nº 002/2020 de 16 de Março—Infeção por SARS-CoV-2 (COVID-19)— Cuidados post mortem, autópsia e casas mortuárias*. https://covid19.min-saude.pt/wp-content/uploads/2020/03/i026008.pdf

Direção Geral de Estatística da República Portuguesa. (1913). *V Recenseamento Geral da População.* https://www.ine.pt/xportal/xmain?xpid=INE&xpgid=censos_historia_pt_1911

Direção Geral de Estatística da República Portuguesa. (1923). *VI Recenseamento Geral da População.* https://www.ine.pt/xportal/xmain?xpid=INE&xpgid=censos_historia_pt_1920

Freire, M. C. (2016, August 12). Já são 300 os monumentos de homenagem aos combatentes. *Diário de Notícias.* https://www.dn.pt/portugal/ja-sao-300-os-monumentos-de-homenagem-aos-combatentes-5334653.html

Funerais laicos ainda são uma minoria. (2010, November 1). *Público.* https://www.publico.pt/2010/11/01/jornal/funerais-laicos-ainda-sao-uma-minoria-20525520

Garnel, M. R. L. (2009). Morte e memória da pneumónica de 1918. In *A Pandemia Esquecida: Olhares comparados sobre a pneumónica 1918–1919* (pp. 221–235). Imprensa de Ciências Sociais.

Jorge, R. (1885). *Hygiene social applicada á nação portugueza.* Imprensa Civilisação.

Liga dos Combatentes. (n.d.). *Museu do Combatente.* https://www.ligacombatentes.org.pt/museus/museu_do_combatente

Passos, B. P. A. (1878). *Um capitulo de hygiene: A incineração dos cadaveres.* Faculdade de Medicina da Universidade do Porto. https://repositorio-aberto.up.pt/handle/10216/16649

Queiroz, F. (1999). Contributo para a história dos cemitérios de Gaia—3ª Parte. *Boletim da Associação Cultural Amigos de Gaia, 47,* 45–57.

Queiroz, F. (2002). *Os Cemitérios do Porto e a arte funerária oitocentista em Portugal: Consolidação da vivência romântica na perpetuação da memória* [PhD Dissertation in Art History]. Faculdade de Letras da Universidade do Porto.

Queiroz, F. (2005). Portugal. In *Encyclopedia of Cremation.* Ashgate.

Queiroz, F. (2016). Cemitérios e(m) cercas conventuais. *Revista de História Da Arte - Série W, 5,* 103–118.

Queiroz, F., & Portela, A. M. (2003). Uma singular obra de azulejaria barroca em Setúbal. *Actas Do II Congresso Internacional Do Barroco.* II Congresso Internacional do Barroco, Porto.

Queiroz, F., & Rugg, J. (2003). The development of cemeteries in Portugal. *Mortality, 8*(2), 113–128.

Relvas, E., & Rijo, D. (2020). "A epidemia reinante". A pneumónica no concelho de Lisboa, 1918. In J. A. G. Ferreira (ed.) *A Gripe Espanhola de 1918* (pp. 161–180). Casa de Sarmento – Centro de Estudos do Património/UMinho.

Santos, P. E. (2019, July 24). Os mortos que a Guerra Colonial deixou para trás. *Notícias Magazine.* https://www.noticiasmagazine.pt/2019/os-mortos-que-a-guerra-colonial-deixou-para-tras/historias/240152/

Salvador, J. M. (2020, June 13). O adeus ao corpo. Como a cremação está a conquistar os portugueses. *Expresso.* https://expresso.pt/sociedade/2020-06-13-O-adeus-ao-corpo.-Como-a-cremacao-esta-a-conquistar-os-portugueses/

Secretariado Nacional da Pastoral da Cultura. (2012). *Catolicismo e outras "Identidades religiosas em Portugal": Todos os resultados do estudo da Universidade Católica.* https://www.snpcultura.org/catolicismo_e_outras_identidades_religiosas_em_portugal.html

Sequeira, Á. (2001). A pneumónica. *Medicina Interna, 8*(1), 49–55.

Sobral, J. M., & Lima, M. L. (2018). A epidemia da pneumónica em Portugal no seu tempo histórico. *Ler História, 73*, 45–66.

Sousa, P. M. de. (2021). *Os Números da Guerra de África.* Editora Guerra & Paz.

Tavares, J. C. M. (2019). Memórias da Grande Guerra: O Memorial Virtual. *IDN - Cadernos, 34*, 147–155.

Tavares, J. M. (2018). Mortos, feridos e desaparecidos. In A. P. Lousada & J. S. Rocha (eds.) *Portugal na 1ª Guerra Mundial. : Uma História Militar Concisa* (pp. 781–792). Comissão Portuguesa de História Militar.

Xisto, B. O. de O. (2012). *"Assunto encerrado"? Atitudes contemporâneas perante a morte e a cremação em Lisboa* [Master Thesis in Social and Cultural Anthropology]. Universidade de Lisboa.

3 Demographic and legal frameworks

Mortality in Portugal

The size of the Portuguese population has remained stable since 1985, when the number of ten million inhabitants was first reached. Population has hovered around ten million every year, with only a small dip to 9.9 million from 1990 to 1994 (FFMS, 2020c). The preliminary results of the 2021 census reveal that the current size of the resident population in Portugal is 10.3 million (Instituto Nacional de Estatística, 2021a), representing a decrease of 2.0% compared to the results of the 2011 census, in which the resident population was 10.5 million (Instituto Nacional de Estatística, 2012b).

The average number of deaths per year has increased slightly, from 93,093 deaths in 1970 (a 10.7 mortality rate) to 111,793 deaths in 2019 (a 10.9 mortality rate). Over the past ten years, the number of deaths has remained relatively stable, hovering between 100,000 and 115,000 deaths per year (FFMS, 2020a)

The leading causes of death in Portugal are circulatory disease (29.0% of deaths in 2018) and malignant tumors (24.6%), followed by respiratory illness (11.7%), digestive illness (4.3%), and diabetes (3.8%) (FFMS, 2020b).

According to the latest available batch of healthcare statistics, which pertains to the year 2018, 62.9% of all illness-related deaths occur in hospital. In 1969, the earliest year for which this batch of statistics is available, only 18.9% of illness-related deaths were occurring in hospital. Like other developed countries, Portugal has experienced a medicalization of death in recent decades, with more and more of its population dying in hospital than at home (Instituto Nacional de Estatística, 2020).

Legal frameworks

There are two main types of legislation pertaining to death and funeral practices in Portugal.

DOI: 10.4324/9781003153689-3

The first type includes the *Lei* (law) and the *Decreto-Lei* (decree-law), both of which are legislative acts. *Leis* and *Decreto-Leis* will legislate in general terms about a specific matter. They may also define sanctions. A *Lei* is issued by the national parliament, while a *Decreto-Lei* is issued by the government. Most of the ordinary laws published in Portugal are of the *Decreto-Lei* type.

The second type is the *Portaria*. A *Portaria* is an administrative act, issued by one or more members of the Government. A *Portaria* will explore a specific matter in-depth; for this reason, a detailed *Portaria* will usually follow a more general *Decreto-Lei*. A *Portaria* is of inferior value to a *Decreto-Lei*, and should not contradict it.

Death registration

Death registration is a multistep process. First, a physician must verify that a death has occurred; other health practitioners cannot legally conduct this verification. Using a dedicated database entitled *Sistema de Informação dos Certificados de Óbito* (SICO), the physician fills in the *Certificado de Óbito* with the relevant personal and medical information, including the cause of death. Once the physician has completed this task, the *Certificado de Óbito* is sent electronically to the civil registry office; the physician then prints two simplified versions of the document: the *Boletim de Óbito*, which is delivered to the family or executor, and the *Guia de Transporte* (Transport Guide), which will allow funeral professionals to transport the body legally. Generally, preparations for the funeral may begin as soon as the family has received the *Boletim de Óbito*.

The family must present the *Boletim de Óbito* at the civil registry office within 48 hours. The civil registry office matches the *Boletim de Óbito* with the *Certificado de Óbito* in the database and registers the death by filling in the *Assento de Óbito*. Once this step has been completed, the family receives a *Certidão de Óbito*. The *Certidão de Óbito* will be necessary to handle the affairs of the deceased; its cost may differ depending on its intended purpose (Secretaria-Geral do Ministério da Justiça, 2020).

Coroner involvement

In atypical cases, the process of registering a death may be more complex and involve other entities, such as the *Ministério Público* (public prosecutor's office). If the physician who verifies the death suspects that a crime has occurred, or cannot ascertain the cause of death at all, they will report this to the *Ministério Público*, who will decide whether to conduct a post-mortem examination. If the *Ministério Público* decides to conduct a post-mortem examination, the body will be transported to the *Instituto Nacional de Medicina Legal e Ciências Forenses* (National Institute of Legal Medicine and Forensic Sciences, commonly abbreviated as INMLCF) to be examined by a coroner. The coroner will then amend the *Certificado de Óbito* filled in by the physician who first verified the death. In cases where a post-mortem examination has taken place, the body cannot undergo thanatopraxy or cremation without explicit permission from the *Ministério Público*.

Bereavement leave

The *Código do Trabalho* (Labor Code) states that family members are allowed time off work to grieve. An individual may take up to five consecutive days off work, depending on the familial relation to the deceased.

Medical or scientific use of cadavers

Organ harvesting from deceased donors is regulated in chapter III of *Lei 12/93*. This law states that citizens and residents in Portugal who have died in the country and who have not expressed their opposition to the *Ministério da Saúde* (Ministry of Health) through the *Registo Nacional de Não Dadores* (National Registry of Non-Donors) are considered to be potential deceased organ donors. In 2019, Portugal had the fourth highest rate of deceased organ donors per million population in the world, at 33.8 per million (IRODaT, 2020). In that year, there were 347 deceased organ donors, which allowed for 795 transplants (IPST, 2020).

If a person dies in hospital and the body exhibits the appropriate age and health characteristics for organ donation, the hospital will investigate whether the person in question has expressed their opposition. This will be done through the *Registo Nacional de Não Dadores*, but also through the family, whose position is also taken into consideration. If there are no objections, a medical team will extract the necessary organs or tissues, taking care not to disfigure the body. Once the organs have been harvested, the body will be transferred to the morgue, where it may be collected by the family (Sociedade Portuguesa da Transplantação, 2014). Funeral preparations may then continue as usual.

The use of cadavers for teaching and scientific research is regulated by *Decree-Law 274/99*. A cadaver may be used for teaching and research purposes when the deceased person has expressly declared this desire. For this purpose, medical schools at universities may conduct their own body donor programs.

Outside of these cases, citizens and residents in Portugal who have died in the country may be subject to the use of their body for teaching and research, under particular circumstances. A dead body may be dissected if it goes unclaimed for 24 hours after the family or executor have been notified of the death, provided that the deceased person has not expressed their opposition to the *Ministério da Saúde*. The extraction of specific tissues or organs for teaching and scientific purposes is also permitted; for this purpose, it is not necessary that a body goes unclaimed, only that the deceased person has not expressed their opposition.

Medical institutions that use a dead body for teaching and research purposes are responsible for all costs associated with its transportation. They are also responsible for returning the body to the family, if possible, or for arranging for its burial or cremation, if not.

Transportation of dead bodies

The transportation of dead bodies by land, within Portuguese borders, follows *Decree-Law 411/98*. As a rule, dead bodies must be transported in appropriate vehicles which are used exclusively for that purpose. In the vast majority of cases, funeral homes will handle the transportation of dead bodies. Typical scenarios include transporting the body from the place of death to the location of the wake, which usually follows, and then to the final site of disposal (e.g. the cemetery or the crematorium). When transporting dead bodies in these circumstances, funeral homes should accommodate them for transport in coffins that suit the final disposal option: wood for burial and cremation, zinc for entombment. Police authorities, or other entities working in cooperation with police authorities, may also handle the transportation of dead bodies under specific circumstances—for instance, if the body cannot be delivered to the family or the funeral home for disposal within the legal timeframe of 72 hours.

The transportation of dead bodies by rail, sea, or air within Portuguese borders is also regulated in *Decree-Law 411/98*. In such cases, the coffin should be accommodated inside a solid box that disguises its appearance; it should be accompanied, also, by an indication to handle with care.

The transportation of dead bodies across international borders follows the 1937 International Convention on the Transport of Corpses, signed into Portuguese law by Decree-Law 417/70, and the 1973 Agreement on the Transfer of Corpses, signed into Portuguese law by Decree 31/79. The 1973 Agreement supersedes the 1937 International Convention in dealings between countries that have ratified both; for those that have not, the 1937 International Convention remains in force.

The 1973 Agreement states that every dead body should be accompanied, while being transported across international borders, by a *laissez-passer* document (referred to as a *livre-trânsito* in Portuguese) issued by the state of departure. The *laissez-passer* document should include, at least, the following information on the deceased person: full name, date and place of death, age at death, and date and place of birth. It should also include the following information related to the transport itself: place of departure, destination, mode of transportation, and itinerary. The body should be transported in a coffin that contains only the body and whatever personal objects are to be buried or cremated with it. The coffin must be watertight and contain, along with the body, some sort of absorbent material. Embalming is not required. In case the person has died of infectious disease, the body should be wrapped in material which has been impregnated with an antiseptic solution. The Agreement does not apply to the transport of cremation ashes across international borders.

The transportation of dead bodies inside the cemetery is carried out in the manner determined by the cemetery administration in the internal regulations.

The transportation of cremation ashes is free of state regulation, provided that it is carried out 'in an appropriate vessel.'

Body disposal

The Portuguese law allows two forms of body disposal, which are defined in the Decree-Law 411/98. These are *burial* (which includes, technically, both burial and entombment) and cremation, which is defined as the 'reduction of a dead body or skeletal remains to ashes.'

Generally, burial and entombment should be conducted in a cemetery (some exceptions apply), and cremation in a crematorium (i.e. pyre cremation is not permitted). Although there are no specific references to practices such as burial at sea, a strict reading of Decree-Law 411/98 would conclude that burial at sea is neither part of the foreseen exceptions (e.g. burial in private chapels) nor comparable to them; as such, it is not permitted.

Bodies should be buried or cremated between 24 and 72 hours after death. If a post-mortem examination has taken place, the applicable timeframe is 48 hours after the examination. All these timeframes may be shortened if the body is considered to represent a danger to public health (e.g. due to infectious disease). Thanatopraxy may be performed as early as six hours after death.

Cemeteries

The construction and organization of Portuguese cemeteries is regulated in two main legal documents: Decreto 44220 of March 3, 1962, which regulates the construction of cemeteries, and Decreto 48770 of November 22, 1968, which sets a model of internal regulations for all public cemeteries to adapt and publish as their own.

The indications of Decree 44220 are explored in-depth in Chapter 9, as they influence the entire functioning of the cemetery, from the amount of burial space needed to serve a specific community to the dimensions to be respected between graves.

As for Decree 48770, this document occupies a complex position in the Portuguese legal system, in the sense that, even though it defines the model of internal regulations for public cemeteries, legislators at the municipal and local level do not necessarily refer back to it when drafting internal regulations for their cemeteries. Part of the reason has to do with the existence of Decree-Law 411/98, which was published 20 years later and brought significant changes to the funeral sector, namely the replacement of lead coffins by zinc coffins, and the shortening of the resting time for temporary graves from five to three years. Decree-Law 411/98 also introduced the concept of aerobic decomposition modules (precast concrete compartments that promote the process of decomposition) which did not exist at all in the 1960s, when Decree 48770 was published. This legal mismatch leads municipal and local legislators to refer directly to the most recent legislation instead of citing Decree 48770, which, although still valid, only applies in situations that do not contradict subsequent legislation.

Regardless of these issues, Decree 48770 is worth mentioning because it was the first document to define what local legislators should take into account when drafting internal cemetery regulations. Even the most basic regulations should always include details such as opening hours, size limits for graves, conditions for exhumation and grave reuse, among others. Although there are many internal regulations that still follow this basic scheme, the tendency today is for these documents to grow in complexity, as cemeteries need to accommodate changes in funeral practice.[1]

Crematoria

Cremation is defined in Decree-Law 411/98 as one of the two possible forms of body disposal allowed in Portugal. When it was issued, this piece of legislation was of the utmost importance, as it marked the recognition of burial and cremation as equally valid practices.

Cremation is legally defined in article 2° of this Decree-Law as the '*reduction of a corpse or skeletal remains to ashes.*' The Decree-Law also states that cremation equipment must obey the rules defined in a *Portaria* issued by the members of Government responsible for the areas of environment, territorial planning, and health. However, this *Portaria* did not exist at the time Decree-Law 411/98 was published, and it still does not exist today, despite the existence of working groups dedicated to the matter (Direção-Geral da Saúde, n.d.).

In practice, there are no regulations on the construction or the activity of crematoria on Portuguese territory, an issue which has been brought to light, due to environmental concerns, by the press and by elected officials (Garcia, 2015; Sá, 2018). Without national regulations, entities that operate cremation equipment, whether for humans or pets, may look to European Union (EU) directives for guidance. However, the pollutant emissions from crematoria are not regulated under EU law: as of August 2019, the regulation of emissions from crematoria is exclusively in the remit of Member States (European Commission, 2019). This legal vacuum is the weak point of cremation in Portugal. Although cremation is defined in this piece of legislation, the document is far from exhaustive; in fact, it places greater emphasis on the handling and disposal of ashes than it does on the cremation process itself. The only article that specifically addresses the cremation process is article 6.°, which states that a body destined for cremation must be transported to the crematorium in a wooden coffin which may be easily destroyed by the action of heat. Effectively, the law does not even state that a body must be cremated *inside* this coffin.

Regarding cremation ashes, Decree-Law 411/98 states ashes may be placed in a cendrarium which, in context, refers to any area or receptacle into which ashes can be stored without individualization: stored in a grave, tomb, ossuary, or columbarium; or delivered to those who have requested the cremation, usually the family. Ashes may be transported freely, both inside and outside the cemetery, as long as this is done 'in an appropriate container.' Families are free to store or dispose of the ashes as they wish; there is no further regulation. Ashes resulting from cremations performed on the initiative of a cemetery administration, such as those of abandoned remains or anatomical specimens, should be placed exclusively in a cendrarium. Cremation may be performed on the recently deceased, on exhumed corpses, on skeletal remains, on dead fetuses, and on anatomical specimens. For the recently deceased, the same conditions apply as for burial: no body can be cremated before 24 hours have passed since the moment of death (article 8.°); likewise, no body can be cremated without its respective *boletim de óbito* (death certificate). The maximum timeframes also apply: a body should be cremated, at most, 72 hours after death or 48 hours after autopsy (article 8.°), if applicable (Nascimento & Trabulo, 2008). All these timeframes may be shortened if it is considered the body represents a danger to public health (e.g. due to an infectious disease).

Cremation, like burial, may be requested, in order: by the executor of the will, by the partner of the deceased (married or not), and by any heirs, any family members, or any person or entity (article 3.°). Previously, cremation could only be requested by specific family members, or by a majority of the heirs, provided that this request did not clash with the explicit will of the deceased. Effectively, Decree-Law 411/98 made it easier for families to request and freely choose cremation, which is coherent with the objective of the legislation, to liberalize cremation and make it fully equal to burial. In the current context, families requesting cremation are not subject to more bureaucracy than families requesting burial. Either service must be requested from the entity responsible for the administration of the cemetery, crematorium, or funerary center where the body will be committed, through a form entitled *Requerimento para Inumação ou Cremação*. This form is administrative in nature and does not require the signature of a healthcare professional.

The funeral profession

Funeral directing in Portugal is regulated by Decree-Law 109/2010, which establishes the regime for access to and exercise of the funeral activity, and Decree-Law 10/2015, which approves the regime for access to and exercise of various trade activities, including the funeral activity. These legal documents define the 'funeral activity' as services related to the organization and realization of funerals, or services related to the transportation, burial, exhumation, cremation, repatriation, and transfer of bodies or remains. In addition to these main services, which make up the *de facto* funeral activity in Portugal, Decree-Law 109/2010 also lists complementary activities that can be practiced by companies in this sector: the preparation and temporary conservation of corpses, the sale of funerary or religious items, or the ornamentation of funeral and religious services, among others.

Funeral directing is practiced by private entities. This includes both funeral homes and IPSS (*Instituições Particulares de Solidarie-dade Social*, Private Social Solidarity Institutions). Mutual aid associations are included among the latter, but they may only provide funeral services to their members, according to Decree-Law 10/2015 (article 110, paragraph 4). Mutual aid associations have around one million members in Portugal, along with two-and-a-half million beneficiaries (members and their families) (União das Mutualidades Portuguesas, 2014).

Article 121 of Decree 10/2015 lists the entities that cannot provide funeral services because it is considered incompatible with their original activity. This includes the managing entities of hospitals and other healthcare institutions, and the managing entities of public cemeteries. IPSS, which are often involved in the management of retirement and care homes for the elderly, are specifically regarded as an exception to this rule (paragraph 2). Thus, the law allows IPSS to provide both healthcare and funeral services. To ensure that IPSS cannot impose their funeral services on their healthcare patients and their families, the law enshrines the 'right of choice' in article 118 of the decree: hospital establishments are prohibited from cooperating with entities providing funeral services for the preferential or exclusive provision of services to their patients.

Funeral homes and mutual aid associations that carry out funeral activities must register with the Directorate-General for Economic Activities (DGAE, from the Portuguese "Direção-Geral das Atividades Económicas"). Likewise, they must have a Technical Manager (*Responsável Técnico*) who has completed a professional course that qualifies them to supervise, plan, and ensure the exercise of funeral activities; have a diversified catalog of funeral items in order to guarantee that customers have options to choose from; guarantee the transport of dead bodies or their remains in conditions of safety and respect for human dignity; ensure that the professionals and equipment for the preparation and preservation of bodies meet the requirements for the practice of thanatopraxy (*Portaria* 162-A/2015 of July 1); own at least one establishment in national territory which is open to the public, equipped with autonomous facilities, and exclusively dedicated to funeral activities.

Note

1 Internal cemetery regulations are publicly accessible and may be found in series II of *Diário da República* ('Diary of the Republic'), the official periodical publication of the Portuguese Republic.

References

Direção-Geral da Saúde. (n.d.). *Crematórios*. https://www.dgs.pt/saude-ambiental/areas-de-intervencao/crematorios.aspx

European Commission. (2019). *Answer Given by Mr Vella on behalf of the European Commission—Question reference: E-002221/2019*. https://www.europarl.europa.eu/doceo/document/E-9-2019-002221-ASW_EN.html

FFMS - Fundação Francisco Manuel dos Santos. (2020a). *Óbitos de residentes em Portugal: Total e no primeiro ano de vida*. PORDATA - Base de Dados de Portugal Contemporâneo. https://www.pordata.pt/Portugal/%c3%93bitos+de+residentes+em+Portugal+total+e+no+primeiro+ano+de+vida-15

FFMS - Fundação Francisco Manuel dos Santos. (2020b). *Óbitos por algumas causas de morte (%)*. PORDATA - Base de Dados de Portugal Contemporâneo. https://www.pordata.pt/Portugal/%c3%93bitos+por+algumas+causas+de+morte+(percentagem)-758

FFMS - Fundação Francisco Manuel dos Santos. (2020c). *População residente, média anual: Total e por grupo etário*. PORDATA - Base de Dados de Portugal Contemporâneo. https://www.pordata.pt/Portugal/Popula%C3%A7%C3%A3o+residente++m%C3%A9dia+anual+total+e+por+grupo+et%C3%A1rio-10

Garcia, R. (2015, November 1). Aumento de cremações é um problema ambiental? *Público*. https://www.publico.pt/sociedade/noticia/do-po-vieste-ao-po-voltaras-1712973

Instituto Nacional de Estatística. (2020). *Estatísticas da Saúde: 2018*. https://www.ine.pt/xurl/pub/257793024

Instituto Nacional de Estatística. (2012a). *Censos 2011 Resultados Definitivos—Portugal*. https://censos.ine.pt/xportal/xmain?xpid=CENSOS &xpgid=ine_censos_publicacao_det&contexto=pu&PUBLICACOES pub_boui=73212469&PUBLICACOESmodo=2&selTab=tab1& pcensos=61969554

Instituto Nacional de Estatística. (2021b). *Resultados Preliminares—Censos 2021*. https://censos.ine.pt/xportal/xmain?xlang=pt&xpgid=censos21_ dados&xpid=CENSOS21

IPST. (2020). *Doação e Transplantação de Órgãos—Atividade Nacional 2019*. http://www.ipst.pt/files/TRANSPLANTACAO/DOACAOETRANS PLANTACAO/Colheita_e_Transplantacao_Dados_Anuais_2019.pdf

IRODaT. (2020). *International Registry on Organ Donation and Transplantation—Final Numbers 2019*. https://www.irodat.org/img/ database/pdf/Newsletter%20Dec%202020%20.pdf

Nascimento, E., & Trabulo, M. (2008). *Cemitérios: Ordenamentos e questões jurídicas*. Almedina.

Sá, N. (2018). *Pergunta 3162/XIII/3—Portaria de regulamentação Decreto-Lei n.º 411/98, de 30 de Dezembro*. https://www.parlamento.pt/Actividade Parlamentar/Paginas/DetalhePerguntaRequerimento.aspx?BID=107434

Secretaria-Geral do Ministério da Justiça. (2020). *Pedir certidão de óbito*. https://justica.gov.pt/Servicos/Pedir-certidao-de-obito

Sociedade Portuguesa da Transplantação. (2014). *Dador Cadáver*. http://www. spt.pt/site/desktop/webpage-23.php

União das Mutualidades Portuguesas. (2014). *Mutualismo*. https://mutualismo. pt/portal/index.php?page=lerContent&idnot=69&tema=Mutualismo #conteudo%202014

4 Governance and professionalization

Cemetery management

The management of active Portuguese cemeteries in the present day holds three distinct realities: it may be public, private, or a public–private partnership. These realities also apply to crematoria across the country (see Chapter 10 for further information).

The vast majority of active Portuguese cemeteries is managed by the public sector at the municipal (*Câmara Municipal*) or local (*Freguesia*) level. Private entities can also manage cemeteries. This includes not only private companies, but also IPSS (*Instituições Particulares de Solidariedade Social*, Private Social Solidarity Institutions). The Lapa Brotherhood, which has managed its own private cemetery in Oporto since the 19th century, is an example of an IPSS. In the very small number of private cemeteries existing in Portugal are also included the ones managed by foreign communities (such as the British).

According to Decree-Law 170/2019, a public–private partnership is a contract between a public entity and a private entity in which the private entity assumes the management of a public infrastructure or public service for a predetermined period of time. *Tanatório de Matosinhos* and Elvas cemetery are two examples of public infrastructures (which, in this case, include cemeteries and crematoria) managed by private entities, which are responsible for their financing, operation, and risk management during the agreed upon timeframe.

With regard to financing, the State does not automatically offer subsidies or financial contributions to municipalities and civil parishes for the specific task of managing public cemeteries. However, the annual state budget may include funds to finance projects that are relevant to regional and local development. In the case of local administrations, this financing can help cover all types of expenses, from personnel expenses to maintenance expenses, including those related to cemeteries. It can also help finance, for example, the construction of new infrastructure, such as mortuary chapels or ossuaries.

DOI: 10.4324/9781003153689-4

Public cemeteries tend to be the most important source of revenue for municipalities and civil parishes (Oliveira, 2015). However, this does not mean that cemeteries are financially self-sustaining. The first reason for this is the fact that local administrations are not obliged to invest cemetery revenue back into the cemetery itself; it may be channeled into other public services. The second reason is of a practical nature: even if cemetery revenue had to be invested back into the cemetery, in some cases, the cost of maintaining the cemetery would still be greater than the revenue generated by fees and concessions.

Cemeteries under public management

For historical reasons, while some municipalities do not own a single cemetery, other municipalities manage not only one or more municipal cemeteries, but also some cemeteries that were previously under local administration at the parish level.

At the lower level of government, local authorities run local cemeteries, with the President of each one being its superior member. The cemetery administrator (usually a single individual) is responsible for assisting the community in any cemetery-related matters, processing all application forms and issuing payment receipts for burials and exhumations, purchases, and other documental matters. This professional also reports any relevant matters related with the cemetery (e.g. damaged graves or complaints) to the Executive Board and the President. The Executive Board, under the President's authority, manages and supervises the staff working at the cemetery, such as gravediggers. Gravediggers are tasked with all the practical tasks that occur around the cemetery, like opening and closing graves for the purpose of burial, exhumation, and transfer. Larger municipalities may have employees whose only job is to perform the role of gravedigger; in smaller localities, however, the employee who performs the role of gravedigger may also carry out a variety of other tasks around the cemetery, usually related to gardening and general maintenance.

At the municipal level, there is greater stratification of duties and hierarchies. Generally, a councilman is the main authority in charge of the municipal cemeteries, issuing and signing all official documents. The cemetery administrators perform the same tasks as they would at the local level, and other professional(s) is(are) nominated for managing the staff working at the cemetery.

Public cemeteries managed by public entities differ from one another in very significant ways, since they each have the authority to publish their own internal regulations—which follow a national model, but may divert from it when appropriate. Some cemeteries may charge families who have graves with a fee for supplying water to the cemetery, or for treating waste disposal. Some cemeteries may also establish burial restrictions according to the deceased's area of residence, or even introduce a legal obligation to purchase the perpetual concession of a grave in order to perform the funeral. From defining specific opening hours to restricting the sort of paraphernalia authorized on the graves, cemeteries have considerable leeway in their internal regulations.

Cemeteries under private management and public–private partnerships

Private cemeteries managed by religious brotherhoods are generally legally integrated into the IPSS that fund them. Religious Brotherhoods such as Irmandade do Bonfim bear specific regulations for their cemetery such as the ability to bury relatives on perpetual graves being restricted to active members of the brotherhood, their spouses, or their descendants.

Private cemeteries owned by foreign communities, on the other hand, can follow completely different forms of management, for almost all were established following special privileges granted during the monarchy period and have now a very small volume of annual burials.

Private entities managing private cemeteries benefit from a level of autonomy and flexibility on certain issues, for instance, the issue of expiry of perpetual concessions due to abandonment. Municipalities and civil parishes, because they are integrated in the public sector, follow specific guidelines on this matter, but private entities do not necessarily have to respect them. This makes it possible for private entities to be more agile in managing situations where concessions expire, for instance.

Public cemeteries under the management of private entities merge some of the features found in both the public and private sectors. Regulations for these cemeteries tend to be more detailed, taking into account future developments and new disposal methodologies. It is possible that private management may be more open to new and alternative ideas and may want to adapt internal regulations in that direction.

An interesting example of a public cemetery under private management is that of the municipal cemetery in Elvas, the management of which was transferred to a private entity in 2007, for a period of 20 years. The media reported that this cemetery would be the first in

Portugal to receive an environmental certification, achieved through a dedication to the use of environmentally friendly materials such as biodegradable coffins ("Cemitério ecológico," 2008; "Único cemitério com certificado ambiental do país," 2009). This would not only make the cemetery more environmentally friendly, but would also speed up decomposition and, as a result, increase the rate of grave turnover. However, the internal regulations for the Elvas cemetery, found under Regulamento n.° 277/2008, are not consistent with all of the statements made in the press. There are no references to environmental concerns anywhere in the document, and the specific provisions that could be considered consistent with the aim of providing environmentally friendly burials are nowhere near as detailed as suggested by the press. For instance, article 20 states that, in perpetual graves, only wooden coffins are allowed, but nothing else is said regarding the materials, construction, and biodegradable quality of these coffins. Despite this incongruity, the Elvas case is a highly visible example of a public cemetery which, under private management, sought to adapt to new disposal methodologies and consumer needs, in this case by promoting the concept of environmentally friendly burials.

A private entity running and managing either a private or public cemetery cannot act fully independently, and consequently, must report and communicate with the appropriate authorities, at the municipal or local level, to require authorization for specific matters (e.g. the cremation of unclaimed bodies or abandoned remains), therefore having as a direct consequence to follow the general law applied to the Portuguese cemeteries.

Differences between public and private management

The reason behind most of what was referred previously is that management strategies for cemeteries in the public sector rely upon a short-term scale, frequently conditioned by the due time of each public office term of four years, whereas private entities responsible for the management of either public or private cemeteries are able to rely on a longer-term scale, depending on the duration of the concession (which may even be permanent).

Apart from national legislation, each cemetery may develop its own internal regulation, which often leads to a discrepancy of certain matters and legal procedures between cemeteries. These distinct matters are related not only with management and maintenance of the Portuguese cemeteries across different regions due to their public, private, or public–private partnership configurations, but also with each local need for adaptation according to each situation and local specifications.

Qualifications and training

In what concerns the training of cemetery staff, the realities are different in the public and private sectors, although the difference has more to do with the nature of each sector than with the nature of cemetery work.

To be able to work in a local or municipal cemetery, a candidate must apply for the job through a public recruitment process. To do this, they must be at least 18 years old and of Portuguese nationality. They must be physically and psychologically able to perform the functions they are applying for, and they must comply with mandatory vaccination laws. Finally, they cannot have been previously prohibited from working in the public sector. There are three distinct careers in the public sector, and jobs associated with cemeteries are integrated into the two careers with the lowest educational requirements. Gravediggers are integrated in the operational assistant (*assistente operacional*) career, which requires that they have completed compulsory education.[1] Cemetery employees who perform administrative functions are part of the technical assistant (*assistente técnico*) career, which requires that they have completed 12th grade. Public recruitment processes are long and go through several stages such as knowledge tests, psychological assessments, and interviews; as such, while previous job experience in a cemetery is rarely required, it will certainly be considered. The recruitment processes for the public sector and respective results are announced in the *Diário da República*, so they are accessible to all citizens. Once a candidate has acquired the job, then the theoretical and practical aspects of the profession may be learned *in loco*.

Cemetery staff working in privately managed or privately owned cemeteries are subject to different requirements, as they are initially hired in recruitment processes that respond to the specific needs of a private employer. Thus, the requirements can be higher from the start. Once an employee has acquired the job, there is theoretical–practical training and internal training of the workforce that compose the different needs of the private cemetery. Because the private sector's economic objective is to make a profit, there is greater investment in training in order to optimize the work of each employee. Each function has a well-defined operations manual that each professional must know and practice. Besides the operations manual and preparation (professional standards for the practicing of a specific job), all employees in the private sector are entitled to a minimum of 40 hours of continuous training, per year, related to the tasks they perform (article 131 Lei 7/2009). Cemetery staff working for a private employer may benefit from training on topics such as customer service, grief psychology, team management, and more. The training itself can be done by trade associations in the funeral sector (see section below), or by certified training centers, depending on the specificity of the topic.

Having looked at the recruitment and training of cemetery staff in the public and private sectors, we can now look into the recruitment and training of the professionals who work in funeral homes. The public–private contrast does not exist here, as all funeral homes belong to the private sector.

The theoretical–practical training and preparation to perform any kind of funeral activity in Portugal is divided into two professional categories, which are required to be able to work in this field: Funeral Director (*Agente Funerário*) and Technical Manager (*Responsável Técnico*). Both are regulated by the norms defined in the National Qualifications Framework, or QNQ, which ranks qualifications from level 1 (basic education) to 8 (doctorate). The Funeral Director training is equivalent to level 2 according to QNQ and has an average total of 1,442 hours. The Technical Manager training is equivalent to level 4 and has an average total of 2,150 hours. According to Decree-Law 109/2010, each funerary agency must have an associated technical manager. Similar to what we see in the privately managed or privately owned cemeteries, the professionals of the funerary sector are required by law to attend 40 hours of training per year related to their job.

Trade associations

The funeral directing industry is represented by four national associations, listed here in order of creation:

- AAFP – Associação de Agentes Funerários de Portugal (Association of Funeral Directors of Portugal). Created in 1988, this was the first association dedicated exclusively to the representation of funeral directors operating in Portugal;
- ANEL – Associação Nacional de Empresas Lutuosas (National Association of Mortuary Companies). Founded in 1990, this is the

largest Portuguese organization of companies in the funeral sector. The association has training as its main priority;
- AAFC – Associação dos Agentes Funerários do Centro (Association of Funeral Directors of Central Portugal). This association was created in 2001 with the objective of representing and defending funeral homes in central Portugal. It has since expanded its scope of action to the entire national territory;
- APPSF – Associação Portuguesa dos Profissionais do Sector Funerário (Portuguese Association of Funeral Sector Professionals). Created in 2005, this association shares leadership with Servilusa. It has the least overlap with the others.

Together, these associations represent 1,500 funeral-related companies across the country, employing a total of 6,000 workers (Esteves, 2019), meaning that each of these companies employ on average four people.

In addition to representing the professional interests of the funeral sector, providing legal support and advice, and contributing to the creation of new legislation, these trade associations also provide training. The AAFP, ANEL, and AAFC all offer training courses of various durations on general topics such as sales techniques, customer service, or marketing, and specific topics such as thanatopraxy, anatomy, funerary legislation, or psychology of grief. In 2008, Servilusa opened its own School of Cemetery Operators near the public cemetery of Elvas, which Servilusa manages. The courses, aimed at both gravediggers and funeral directors, are taught by the APPSF, a trade association that shares leadership with Servilusa (Antunes, 2008).

Note

1 For more information on gravediggers as human resources, see Jacques (2012).

References

Antunes, M. (2008, April 23). Escola ensina a trabalhar com a morte. *Expresso Emprego*. https://expressoemprego.pt/noticias/escola-ensina-a-trabalhar-com-a-morte/1919

Cemitério ecológico. (2008, May 6). http://www.tvi24.iol.pt/elvas/ambiente/cemiterio-ecologico

Jacques, M. H. G. (2012). *Os Coveiros enquanto Recursos Humanos* [Master Thesis in Management of Human Resources]. Instituto Superior de Línguas e Administração.

Oliveira, J. C. C. R. de. (2015). *"Direito Mortuário" e Finanças Locais: A gestão de cemitérios enquanto receita das Autarquias Locais* [Master Thesis in Local Government Law]. Universidade do Minho.

Único cemitério com certificado ambiental do país. (2009, October 28). http://www.industriaeambiente.pt/scid/webIA/defaultArticleView One.asp?categoryID=780&articleID=518

5 Religion and funerary practice

Religious history

Christianity was introduced to what is now Portugal under the Roman Empire; as such, when Portugal was officially founded in 1143, it was founded as a Christian kingdom. The consequent expansion of the kingdom of Portugal toward the south of the Iberian Peninsula was as important politically as it was religiously: as Portugal expanded south, it furthered the Christianization and de-Islamization of the Iberian Peninsula. This symbiosis between Church and State would shape the relationship between the Portuguese state and the Catholic Church for centuries to come. At the same time, it would have enormous influence on the country's religious demographics: although Portugal was, in its early history, home to Islamic and Jewish communities, these communities were persecuted over the centuries, culminating in the forced conversion of the Jews from Portugal in the late 15th century. With the exception of the Jewish community of Belmonte, there is hardly a connection to be drawn, today, between the contemporary and the early Islamic and Jewish presence in Portugal.

Like other countries in southern Europe, Portugal remained faithful to the Catholic Church through the Reformation. Following the Catholic Counter-Reformation and the action of the Inquisition, especially from the end of the 16th century, religious beliefs other than Catholicism were no longer tolerated in the country. An exception was made for British merchants, whose freedom of religion—provided they were discreet—was secured in international treaties between England and Portugal over the 17th century (which, in turn, only existed because of the Treaty of Windsor, an alliance signed between the two countries in 1373). Between the 17th and 18th centuries, there was no formal place of worship in Portugal that was not Catholic. Even burial places with a non-Catholic rite only came to be built in the 18th century on the condition they would not be visible from the street.

DOI: 10.4324/9781003153689-5

From the 18th century onward, secularism and anti-Clericalism began to take root among intellectual elites. The Inquisition would be abolished in 1821, signaling a new dawn of religious tolerance. From the 1820s onward, non-Catholic worship became acceptable in Portugal, provided that it was done discreetly and by foreign communities. Jewish families coming from Gibraltar and Morocco began to settle in Portugal during this period.

In order to fully separate State and Church, the first republican government issued the *Lei da Separação do Estado das Igrejas* (Law of Separation) on April 20, 1911. Catholicism was demoted from state religion and became just another option among many. Previously, only the Catholic Church had been allowed to build temples with outward religious symbols—now, that freedom was extended to all religions. Radical as they may have been, these changes did not produce long-term effects; two decades later, another regime shift would revert the anticlerical stance of the First Republic and embrace Catholicism (albeit with limitations) once again.

Figure 5.1 One of the tombs of the Danish family Andresen, in the former non-Catholic section at Agramonte, Oporto, during a nocturnal photography scavenger hunt.

The *Estado Novo* regime, which held power from 1932 to 1974, re-established the importance of Catholicism in cultural and societal terms, but did not restore its status as the state religion. The regime embraced the interests of the Catholic Church and worked to mend the relationship between Portugal and the Holy See, which the First Republic had damaged with radical anticlerical measures. The relationship would be formally established in a Concordat signed between Portugal and the Holy See of the Catholic Church in 1940.

Under the Concordat of 1940, Portugal recognized the Catholic Church as the traditional religion of the Portuguese people. The state would remain secular and the Church would hold limited autonomy—e.g. the government would vet the nomination of Bishops and Archbishops. In turn, the state agreed to the teaching of Catholic religion and moral in public schools, asylums, and orphanages, among a series of other privileges. In essence, the Catholic Church was not the official state religion, but was the only religion actively endorsed by the state. Portuguese society was indoctrinated into the Catholic Church and, as a result, the process of secularization which the First Republic had begun could not continue.

After 1974, with the Third Republic, the separation of Church and State was fully enshrined in the Constitution: according to article 41°, paragraph 4, churches and other religious communities are separate from the state and are free to organize themselves and to exercise their functions and form of worship. The *Lei da Liberdade Religiosa* (Law of Religious Freedom), issued in 2001, expands on the subject of the neutrality of the state: Portugal does not have an official religion, nor does it promote any specific religious guidelines. Theoretically, this should mean the Catholic Church does not benefit from any legal privileges denied to other religious denominations; however, the fact that Portugal and the Holy See of the Catholic Church hold diplomatic as well as religions relationship means some privileges may be awarded based on international treaties, such as the Concordat of 2004. In the realm of funerary practice, for instance, bishops may still be buried inside cathedrals, which is contrary to the spirit of the 1835 law.

Religious demographics

At the 2011 census (Instituto Nacional de Estatística, 2012), 81% of the Portuguese population identified their religion as Catholic. Around 7% of respondents stated they had no religion, and 4% stated they practiced another religion. The remaining 8% did not answer the question.

Table 5.1 Religious affiliation according to the census, 2011 (percentage)

Catholic	81.00
Did not respond	8.29
No religion	6.84
Other Christian	1.82
Protestant	0.84
Orthodox	0.63
Other non-Christian	0.32
Muslim	0.23
Jewish	0.03

Source: Based on Instituto Nacional de Estatística (2012) *Censos 2011 Resultados Definitivos— Portugal.* https://censos.ine.pt/xportal/xmain? xpid=CENSOS&xpgid=ine_censos_publica- cao_det&contexto=pu&PUBLICACOESpub_ boui=73212469&PUBLICACOESmodo=2&selT- ab=tab1&pcensos=61969554

Apart from the communities that we explore in-depth in this chapter, other religious communities have developed in Portugal since 1974, with the fall of the *Estado Novo* regime and the legal acceptance of all religious denominations. Jehovah's Witnesses and the Mormon church began to practice openly in the 1970s. Evangelical churches such as the Universal Church of the Kingdom of God (IURD), originating from Brazil, then began to gain traction in the 1980s (Faria, 2017). Immigration from Ukraine in the 1990s also contributed to the establishment of Eastern Orthodox communities. In the 21st century, immigration from China to Portugal has also become significant. This community is still very young, however, and it has not yet made an impact on religious or funeral practices in the country. Until this point, these communities have not experienced the same challenges regarding religious freedom, nor had the same impact on Portuguese funerary practice, as the communities we examine in this chapter.

Catholic funerary practice in Portugal

Despite the ongoing legal effort to separate Church and State, Catholicism remains entrenched in Portuguese society. Of the 14 national holidays celebrated in Portugal, nine are Catholic; the other five are political holidays. Cities are entitled to one holiday each, known as *feriado municipal*, and many choose to celebrate theirs on the feast day of a saint. Catholic processions and pilgrimages remain an integral part of Portuguese life in other parts of the country. In May and October, the sanctuary of Our Lady of Fátima welcomes thousands of pilgrims in a widely publicized national event.

Studies suggest the Portuguese identify themselves as Catholic due to a sense of cultural belonging rather than a measure of active religiosity. A study conducted in 2011 found that only 36.2% of Portuguese Catholics attended Mass at least once a week (Secretariado Nacional da Pastoral da Cultura, 2012). Only 56.1% of Portuguese Catholics self-identified as 'practicing,' the lowest figure out of every religion included in the study. The same study showed that, regardless of the religion practiced by the respondents at the time of the study, 87.9% had been baptized in the Catholic faith, and 50.1% had also married in the Catholic rite. This lends credence to the idea that most of the Portuguese population identifies as culturally, rather than religiously, Catholic.

The fact that the Portuguese resort to the Catholic Church in milestones such as births and marriages means that they also resort to the Catholic Church for funerals. In 2010, 80%–90% of all funerals were Catholic ("Funerais Laicos Ainda São Uma Minoria," 2010). With this in mind, we quickly realize Catholicism holds a near-monopoly over Portuguese funerary practices: in many ways, Portuguese funerary practice is Catholic funerary practice.

Traditionally, the Roman Catholic Church privileges burial over other forms of body disposal. The Catholic Church only lifted the ban on cremation in 1963, stating that burial would still be preferable, but cremation would be allowed as long as it was not done to express a refusal to believe in the resurrection of the body. Portugal did not fully embrace the practice of cremation until the 1990s.

We may consider the emergence of cremation one of the most significant disruptors to Catholic funerary practice in Portugal, second only to the tumultuous relationship between Church and State during the creation of public cemeteries in the 19th century. Even so, the country has had no trouble accommodating the recommendations of the Church regarding cremation. In practical terms, the Catholic Church requires that cremation ashes are preserved with reverence, in cemeteries or other pre-approved sacred places; in 2016, the Vatican clarified this position, reiterating that scattering ashes is not permitted (Congregation for the Doctrine of the Faith, 2016). This recommendation is fully accommodated by Portuguese law, which does not force families to keep ashes in cemeteries, but does offer multiple options for the storage of cremation ashes in cemeteries for those who wish to do so.

Among the many Christian holidays celebrated in Portugal is *Dia de Todos os Santos* (All Saints' Day) on November 1. It is customary for mourners to visit the graves of their loved ones on this date. Families may visit multiple graves on the same day and decorate them lavishly. Caring for graves is generally a domestic affair, taken care of by the women in the family.

Even within the larger context of Catholic practice, there is room for some variation. For instance, the Roma community, which in Portugal comprises approximately 40,000 people, participates in the traditional Catholic rituals but instills them with a greater sense of communal loss. Funerals can be very large and crowded, and it is not uncommon for women to externalize their grief by keening and wailing. Typically, the Roma reject cremation in favor of burial and insist on spending time near the grave of the deceased. In some cases, this translates into daily visits to the grave and in others, it takes the form of a particular tradition where families spend the entirety of All Saints' Day at the cemetery (ADCMoura, 2013; 'Ciganos Da Chamusca...' 2018; Mendes, 2002).

Protestant funerary practice in Portugal

The impact of the Protestant Reformation in Portugal, a traditionally Catholic country, was extremely low. Protestantism was mainly imported into the country by British merchants, who began to establish influential communities in the 18th century. These communities would build the country's first (and so far, only) Protestant cemeteries in the 19th century.

Despite the fact that Portugal was a Catholic country with an active Inquisition persecuting 'heresy,' the freedom of religion for British subjects living in the country was secured in writing, starting from the Anglo-Portuguese peace and commercial treaty signed in 1642. The condition was that they practice their religion in private, in their own homes. The Anglo-Portuguese treaty of 1642 stated that the British should not be inconvenienced because of their religion, as long as they did not cause any kind of scandal. A second treaty, signed in 1654, allowed British subjects to have their own chaplains and added that they should be given a place to bury their dead.

Until then, British subjects, due to their heretical beliefs, had not been able to bury their dead in the existing Catholic *adros*. In Lisbon and Oporto, the British were buried in unmarked graves on unconsecrated land, on the south banks of the Tejo and Douro rivers, respectively.

Portuguese authorities finally allowed the British community to lease or purchase land to establish cemeteries in the 18th century.

The British Cemetery of Lisbon, sometimes known as St. George's Cemetery, was established in 1717 (Queiroz, 2014). When the Dutch Protestant community purchased an adjacent plot for the same purpose, the two burial grounds were walled in together. Into the 20th century, the cemetery also came to house Commonwealth War Graves from World War II. In Oporto, the British Cemetery was established in the 1780s. Like in Lisbon, the cemetery came to serve Protestants of other nationalities, namely German and Dutch (Queiroz, 2006). Both cemeteries remain in use today and the later may be considered the first cemetery, in the true sense of the word, ever built in Portugal.

In both cities, the construction of Protestant cemeteries preceded the construction of Protestant churches; the Lisbon community built the Church of St. George, adjacent to the cemetery, in 1822, and the Oporto community completed the Church of St. James, also adjacent to the cemetery, in 1818 (Queiroz, 2006, 2014). Both churches are located within the walls of the cemetery; like the cemeteries themselves, they are not visible from the street. In order to be authorized, these Anglican chapels had to comply with some restrictions, namely that of not having a bell tower.

Figure 5.2 British Cemetery of Lisbon.

Jewish funerary practice in Portugal

There are two types of Jewish communities in Portugal: the Sephardic Jewish community of Belmonte, which dates back to at least the 13th century, and the Jewish communities of Lisbon, Oposto, Faro (now mostly extinct), and the Azores, which began to form after the abolition of the Inquisition in 1821. The size of these communities is reflected in the 2011 census, where 3,061 people, or 0.03% of the Portuguese population, marked their religion down as Jewish. Of these, 884 lived in the Lisbon metropolitan area, and 298 in the Oporto metropolitan area. In Belmonte, 66 people marked their religion down as Jewish.

Current members of the Sephardic Jewish community of Belmonte are descendants of Crypto-Jews who converted to Catholicism but continued to adhere to Judaism in private during the Inquisition. The community did not resume the public practice of Judaism until the late 20th century. It was officially recognized in 1989. The Beit Eliahu synagogue was inaugurated in 1996, and the Jewish cemetery in 2001 (Rede de Judiarias de Portugal, n.d.). Prior to that, the Jewish community had buried their dead in the public cemetery next door (Felizardo, 2001). The new cemetery includes a tahara house attached to the burial ground, meant for the washing and preparation of the body.

The Jewish community of Lisbon began to form in the first half of the 19th century, and permission for the construction of the first Jewish cemetery in the city was granted by King Luís I in 1868. Prior to that, the community had buried their dead in a small plot adjacent to the British Cemetery (Comunidade Israelita de Lisboa, n.d.-b). In 1892, the community founded a mutual aid association called Guemilut Hassadim. The society was created to conduct funeral rites, handle burials, and administer the two cemeteries used by the community: the official Jewish cemetery created in 1868, and the older plot near the British Cemetery. The Shaaré Tikvá synagogue in Lisbon was inaugurated in 1904. The community would only be granted official recognition as the Comunidade Israelita de Lisboa in 1912, in the early years of the First Republic. Today, the Jewish community in Lisbon also has access to other synagogues, such as the Ohel Jacob synagogue, the first Ashkenazi synagogue in the country.

Oporto had been home to some Jewish families (both Sephardic and Ashkenazi) in the 19th century, but the community only organized in the 1920s, when Portuguese army captain Artur Carlos de Barros Bastos, who had recently converted to Judaism, made a concerted effort to form a Jewish community in the city (Vasconcelos,

2019). The *Comunidade Israelita do Porto* was registered in 1923, and the Kadoorie synagogue was inaugurated in 1938. Despite being the largest synagogue in the Iberian Peninsula (Davidson, n.d.), for most of the 20th century, it served only a few families of central and eastern European origin. Today, it serves a much larger Jewish community, with members of various national origins. Unlike the communities in Lisbon and Belmonte, the community of Oporto does not yet have a dedicated cemetery. The construction of a Jewish cemetery in Maia, in the outskirts of Oporto, is underway; according to Rabbi Daniel Litvak of the Kadoorie synagogue (personal communication), the cemetery will feature a tahara room and a dedicated space for funeral speeches.

Jewish communities typically resort to chevra kadisha, a Jewish burial society consisting of volunteers, to prepare the body for burial. Both the Lisbon and Oporto communities have their own chevra kadisha (European Jewish Congress, n.d.). According to Rabbi Daniel Litvak (personal communication), the funerary practice of the Jewish Portuguese community does not differ significantly from that observed in other countries. Immediately after the death, the eyes of the deceased should be closed and the body should be covered with a white sheet. The body of the deceased should not remain alone. It is customary for members of the chevra kadisha of the same gender as the deceased to perform the tahara, the washing and purifying of the body, before burial. Once the body is dried, it is wrapped in a white linen shroud; then, the eyes of the deceased are covered with soil from Israel. The funeral itself is brief. There are opening prayers, a eulogy (*hesped*), and a closing prayer. Upon reaching the burial site, the body is lowered into the grave, and it is customary for each person present to throw three handfuls or three shovels of earth over the grave. The body should remain buried perpetually (Fernandes & Bilro, 2018).

The Jewish community places great value on burying the body on the day of death; however, as we have seen, Portuguese law doesn't allow for burials to be conducted before 24 hours have passed since the death. Jewish custom also forbids autopsies and the donation of bodies to science. Cremation is also prohibited.

According to Jewish custom, one acquires the formal status of mourner when their spouses, parents, siblings, or children die. Immediately following the burial, a Jewish mourner enters a seven-day period of mourning called shiva. During this period, every mourner must perform the kriah, or the act of tearing one's clothes (usually by placing a vertical tear on the lapel of the jacket or shirt). According to Rabbi Daniel Litvak, the custom today is that the Ashkenazi perform the kriah in the cemetery, next to the body of the deceased, while the Sephardi perform the kriah after leaving the cemetery and arriving at the house of mourning. The clothes of the kriah must be worn during all seven days of the shiva period. However, there are variations due to the different levels of religiosity of each family.

Of all the communities explored in this chapter, the Jewish communities have the most cemeteries to their name: two in Lisbon, three in the Azores (in the city of Horta, island of Faial; in the city of Angra do Heroísmo, island of Terceira; and in the city of Ponta Delgada, island of São Miguel), and one in Belmonte. There is also a deactivated Jewish cemetery in Faro. The *Antigo Cemitério da Colónia Judaica de Faro* (Old Cemetery of the Jewish Colony of Faro) was used for about a century, from 1838 to 1932 (Direção-Geral do Património Cultural, n.d.). It was restored in 1984 and it is now musealized.

Figure 5.3 The Jewish Cemetery of Faro.

Hindu funerary practice in Portugal

The 2011 census includes the Hindu community in the 'Other Non-Christian' group. For this reason, it is not possible to say how many census respondents identified their religion as Hindu. In 2017, the press estimated that Portugal was home to 6,000 Hindus (Guedes, 2017)—approximately 0.06% of the population.

Like the Muslim community, the Portuguese Hindu community originated in the migration movements of post-revolutionary Portugal in the 1970s. The first members of the community were immigrants from Mozambique and India, specifically the formerly colonized state of Gujarat, who reside mostly in the Lisbon and Oporto metropolitan areas (Comunidade Hindu de Portugal, 2011). Today, the community also includes local followers of Hare Krishna and members of Nepalese origin (RTP Ensina, 2002). The community began to organize in the 1980s with the creation of the *Associação Hindu de Portugal* (Hindu Association of Portugal). In 1989, the Associação began the construction of the *Complexo da Comunidade Hindu de Portugal*, which would include the Radha-Krishna temple as well as a variety of other spaces of social and cultural relevance to the community (Comunidade Hindu de Portugal, 2011). The Hindu community has worked closely with official entities to make sure that its needs are accommodated: Gujarati, the main language spoken by the community, is taught on Saturdays in municipal schools with the permission of the Ministry of Education. The community has also partnered with the Portuguese Red Cross and the Instituto Português do Sangue to organize blood donation drives in honor of the birthday of Mahatma Gandhi.

In Oporto, the community is represented by the *Associação Cultural Hindu do Porto* (Hindu Cultural Association of Oporto), which was created in 1975 to organize cultural, religious, educational, social, recreational activities of the Hindu and Indian tradition in the city.

The dynamic character of the Hindu community made it instrumental in the reactivation of the Alto de São João crematorium in 1985. The crematorium, which had been built in 1925, had been inactive since 1936; however, the community had a need for it, as according to Hindu tradition, dead bodies must be cremated. Traditionally, the ashes should then be scattered in the Ganges river.

The Hindu community took the first steps to access cremation in 1976, when they tried to obtain permission to cremate one of their members (Dias, 2009, pp. 218–219). The permission was not initially granted, under the argument that cremation was illegal and that it would be better to repatriate the deceased to have him cremated elsewhere. The community insisted: cremation was not illegal, it was merely inaccessible since the only crematorium in the country was inactive. Seemingly in accordance to this, the permission was finally granted, and the community was allowed to cremate the deceased in a wooden pyre during off-hours (Dias, 2009, Monteiro, 2007).

The matter of cremation is perhaps the most relevant matter when it comes to Hindu funerary practices in Portugal. However, another issue comes up, which is the matter of timings. The Hindu community believes the funeral should be arranged as soon as possible after death, but this is not possible according to Portuguese law, which establishes that bodies cannot be cremated until 24 hours after death.

Limited information is available on Hindu funeral rituals in Portugal. When a death occurs, it is traditional for the body to be transported to the family home. There, the body is bathed by people of the same gender as the deceased. Then, a ceremony takes place, after which it is customary for widows to remove their bangles and break them as a sign of respect for their deceased husband. The body remains at home until it must be transported to the crematorium (wood pyre cremations were exceptionally done during the period when there were no active crematoria, but are no longer permitted today). Once the body has been cremated, the ashes are given to the family to be thrown into the river together with flowers, according to tradition (Fernandes & Bilro, 2018). There are records of families transporting the ashes back to India for scattering in the Ganges river; in Lisbon, ashes are occasionally scattered in the Tejo river (Kendall 1997, as cited in Borges, 2012). In Oporto, they are more likely to be stored in the cemetery (Branco, 2015).

Muslim funerary practice in Portugal

According to the 2011 census, 68.81% of the respondents who identified as Muslim lived in Lisbon. The first Muslims to arrive in the country in the 1950s were Sunni Muslims from Mozambique, originally from India, who settled in Lisbon. It was this small group that went on to found the *Comunidade Islâmica de Lisboa* (Islamic Community of Lisbon), in 1968. The community grew significantly in the 1970s, when the *Estado Novo* dictatorial regime fell and gave way to a wave of immigration from the formerly colonized countries to Portugal; among these immigrants were large groups of Muslims from Mozambique and Guinea-Bissau. Throughout the 1980s, three mosques were built in the district of Lisbon: one in Laranjeiro, which opened in 1982; one in Odivelas, which opened in 1983; and, finally, the *Mesquita Central* (Central Mosque) edified by the Islamic Community of Lisbon, which opened in 1985 (Tiesler, 2000). This mosque, along with the Islamic Community of Lisbon that stands behind it, serves both Portuguese citizens and immigrants from a variety of ethnic origins. Despite the fact that smaller mosques and places of worship are spread out throughout the country, the Islamic Community of Lisbon plays a central role in the organization of the Islamic community in Portugal.

Shia Muslims are also present in Portugal, in the form of a Lisbon-based Ismaeli community. The Ismaeli community in Lisbon is ethnically Indian, originating, for the most part, from the Gujarat. They are based in the Ismaeli Center, which was built in the late 1990s.

Northern Portugal is home to 10.96% of the respondents who identified as Muslim. The *Centro Cultural Islâmico do Porto* (Islamic Cultural Center of Oporto) was founded in 1999 (Moreira, 2019); however, the community had been forming since the 1980s. Like the community in Lisbon, the community in Oporto is ethnically heterogeneous, including individuals from Bangladesh, Guinea-Bissau, Senegal, India, and Pakistan. Like in Lisbon, Portuguese Muslims and immigrants frequent the same places of worship.

The funerary practices of the Muslim community differ slightly from city to city, with funerary practices in Lisbon reflecting a greater centralization. Indeed, the Islamic Community of Lisbon is home to a *Comissão de Assuntos Funerários* (Commission for Funerary Matters), which serves the community by supporting families during the mourning period and guaranteeing that funerals follow Shariah law (Fernandes, 2015). In Lisbon, the bodies are typically transported to the mosque, where they are washed, according to Islamic tradition, by family members of the same gender as the deceased. The body is wrapped in a shroud, and a prayer is said for the deceased. The body remains in the mosque overnight, and it is common for the family to stay to watch over it. Afterward, the body is placed inside the coffin and transported to the cemetery for burial. According to Muslim belief, the body should be buried as quickly as possible; under no circumstance should it be cremated. In Lisbon, the community buries their dead in designated areas of the municipal cemeteries of Lumiar, Odivelas, Feijó, and Carnide, which were assigned to the Islamic Community of Lisbon and the Ismaeli Center upon request. According to Sheikh David Munir of the Central Mosque (personal communication), the body should be positioned in the grave so that their right side faces Mecca. The body of each individual must remain buried in the same place in perpetuity, but it is not customary to mark the place with tombstones or flowers. However, according to Sheikh David Munir, there is variation among community members, and there are those who are beginning to adopt the Portuguese custom of placing a monument on the grave. This variation also applies to the 40-day mourning period that is traditional to Islam; during this period, some families may visit the grave every day, although this depends on the level of religiosity of the family.

According to Islamic tradition, it is preferred for the body to be buried in a shroud, but Portuguese law does not state whether this is permissible. The assumption is that a body will be buried inside a coffin, but in practice, it falls on cemeteries to clarify this in their own internal regulations. This loophole has made it possible for Islamic communities to bury their dead without coffins, if so intended; the body is transported in the coffin, removed for burial, and then the coffin is destroyed inside the cemetery ("Muçulmanos: Lei portuguesa exige caixão desnecessário no islamismo," 2009). In choosing this option, the Muslim community tends to choose the most affordable coffins; this, along with the fact that the community prepares their own dead for burial, arranges their own religious ceremonies, and may even backfill the grave after burial, makes the Muslim community largely independent of the funeral sector, which is hired only to transport the bodies and handle bureaucratic matters.

In Oporto, the funeral ritual is similar to Lisbon, but the bodies tend to be buried in wood coffins (Branco, 2015). The community has been requesting a plot in a cemetery for years, in order to allow for the burial of members of the community in the appropriate orientation toward Mecca, but the request has yet to be granted (Ribeiro & Jorge, 2020). In Oporto, it used to be common for Muslim immigrants, particularly from Bangladesh and Guinea-Bissau, to request the repatriation of the body back to the country of origin. This practice may be time-consuming and go against the Muslim belief that the body should be buried as quickly as possible. For this reason, this practice is controversial among Portuguese Muslims (Mapril, 2009).

The issue of timings is another point where Muslim communities are not fully accommodated by Portuguese funerary law. Decree-Law 411/98 establishes that bodies must be buried within 24–72 hours after burial. To Muslim communities, however, anything that may delay the moment of burial is seen as undesirable (Abranches, 2007; Branco, 2015).

References

Abranches, M. (2007). *Pertenças Fechadas em Espaços Abertos – Estratégias de (Re)construção Identitária de Mulheres Muçulmanas em Portugal* [ISCTE – Instituto Universitário de Lisboa]. https://www.om.acm.gov.pt/documents/58428/179891/13_MA.pdf/625c9d4c-1cb7-40b4-b4fd-9a2a4f30f9e7

ADCMoura. (2013). *Observatório Sócio-demográfico das comunidades Ciganas.* https://www.adcmoura.pt/Docs/Observatorio_Escolhas.pdf

Borges, P. J. T. (2012). *Cuidados de Saúde e Práticas Hindus* [Faculdade de Teologia da Universidade Católica Portuguesa]. https://repositorio.ucp.pt/bitstream/10400.14/15491/1/Cuidados%20de%20Sa%C3%BAde%20e%20Pr%C3%A1ticas%20Hindus.pdf

Branco, V. R. P. A. (2015). *Religião e Medicina Legal – Três estudos de caso na cidade do Porto.* Instituto de Ciências Biomédicas Abel Salazar da Universidade do Porto.

Câmara já tem terreno para novo tanatório. (2016, August 16). *Maia Primeira Mão.* https://www.primeiramao.pt/sociedade/camara-ja-terreno-novo-tanatorio/

Ciganos da Chamusca e a tradição de passar o Dia de Todos os Santos no cemitério. (2018, November 14). *O Mirante.* https://omirante.pt/semanario/2018-11-08/sociedade/2018-11-07-Ciganos-da-Chamusca-e-a-tradicao-de-passar-o-Dia-de-Todos-os-Santos-no-cemiterio

Comunidade Hindu de Portugal. (2011, June 20). *Quem Somos.* https://www.comunidadehindu.org/quem-somos/

Comunidade Israelita de Lisboa. (n.d.-a). *Actividades e Serviços—Cemitério.* https://cilisboa.org/actividades-e-servi%C3%A7os/cemit%C3%A9rio/

Comunidade Israelita de Lisboa. (n.d.-b). *Quem Somos.* https://cilisboa.org/quem-somos/

Congregation for the Doctrine of the Faith. (2016). *Instruction Ad resurgendum cum Christo Regarding the Burial of the Deceased and the Conservation of the Ashes in the Case of Cremation.* https://www.vatican.va/roman_curia/congregations/cfaith/documents/rc_con_cfaith_doc_20160815_ad-resurgendum-cum-christo_en.html

Davidson, L. (n.d.). *Kadoorie – Mekor Haim.* Synagogues360°. https://synagogues-360.anumuseum.org.il/gallery/kadoorie-mekor-haim/

Dias, N. M. F. (2009). *Remigração e Etnicidade: Mobilidade Hindu No Trânsito Colonial Entre a África de Leste e a Europa.* Instituto de Ciências Sociais da Universidade de Lisboa.

Direção-Geral do Património Cultural. (n.d.). *Antigo cemitério da colónia judaica de Faro.* http://www.patrimoniocultural.gov.pt/pt/patrimonio/patrimonio-imovel/pesquisa-do-patrimonio/classificado-ou-em-vias-de-classificacao/geral/view/74875

European Jewish Congress. (n.d.). *Portugal.* https://eurojewcong.org/communities/portugal/

Faria, N. (2017, October 31). Minorias protestantes em Portugal formam um puzzle em contínuo crescimento. *Público*. https://www.publico.pt/2017/10/31/sociedade/noticia/minorias-protestantes-em-portugal-formam-um-puzzle-em-continuo-crescimento-1790781

Felizardo, S. (2001). Cemitério dignifica Comunidade Judaica. *URBI et ORBI - Jornal Universitário Da Beira Interior*. http://www.urbi.ubi.pt/010220/edicao/55reg_judeus.html

Fernandes, C. A. da S. (2015). *Solidariedade prática. As relações de apoio entre a Comunidade Islâmica de Lisboa e os guineenses* [ISCTE – Instituto Universitário de Lisboa]. https://repositorio.iscte-iul.pt/bitstream/10071/10981/1/Solidariedade%20pr%C3%A1tica.%20As%20rela%C3%A7%C3%B5es%20de%20apoio%20entre%20a%20Comunidade%20Isl%C3%A2mica%20de%20Lisboa%20e%20os%20guineenses.%20-%20C%C3%A1tia%20Alexandra%20da%20Silva%20Fernandes.pdf

Fernandes, A. J., & Bilro, V. (2018, June). Respeito pela diversidade de religiões, de fé e de rituais. *I-Nova*.

Funerais laicos ainda são uma minoria. (2010, November 1). *Público*. https://www.publico.pt/2010/11/01/jornal/funerais-laicos-ainda-sao-uma-minoria-20525520

Garcia, M. A. (2002). *Comunidades marranas nas Beiras*. BOCC - Biblioteca Online de Ciências Da Comunicação Da Universidade Da Beira Interior. http://www.bocc.ubi.pt/pag/garcia-antonieta-comunidades-marranas.html

Guedes, N. (2017, January 10). De Moçambique a fundador da Dan Cake e da Comunidade Hindu de Portugal. *TSF Rádio Notícias*. https://www.tsf.pt/economia/de-mocambique-a-fundador-da-dan-cake-e-da-comunidade-hindu-de-portugal-5596298.html

Instituto Nacional de Estatística. (2012). *Censos 2011 Resultados Definitivos— Portugal*. https://censos.ine.pt/xportal/xmain?xpid=CENSOS&xpgid=ine_censos_publicacao_det&contexto=pu&PUBLICACOESpub_boui=73212469&PUBLICACOESmodo=2&selTab=tab1&pcensos=61969554

Mapril, J. (2009). "Aqui ninguém reza por ele!" Trânsitos fúnebres entre o Bangladesh e Portugal. *Horizontes Antropológicos, 15*(31), 219–239.

Mendes, M. M. (2002). *Um olhar sobre a identidade e a alteridade: Nós, os Ciganos e os Outros, os Não Ciganos*. IV Congresso Português de Sociologia, Lisboa. https://aps.pt/wp-content/uploads/2017/08/DPR462dca6711183_1.pdf

Monteiro, I. (2007). *Ser Mãe Hindu: Práticas e Rituais Relativos à Maternidade e aos Cuidados à Criança na Cultura Hindu em Contexto de Imigração* [Universidade Aberta]. https://www.om.acm.gov.pt/documents/58428/179891/9_IM.pdf

Moreira, C. F. (2019, May 6). Comunidade islâmica quer rezar em novas mesquitas. *Público*. https://www.publico.pt/2019/05/06/local/noticia/mesquitas-porto-sintra-1871414

Muçulmanos: Lei portuguesa exige caixão desnecessário no islamismo. (2009, April 16). *Visão*. https://visao.sapo.pt/lusa/2009-04-16-muculmanos-lei-portuguesa-exige-caixao-desnecessario-no-islamismof504830/

Queiroz, F. (2006). O cemitério britânico do Porto: Elementos históricos e artísticos para um estudo monográfico. *Boletim Da Associação Cultural Amigos Do Porto*, *3*(24), 119–157.

Queiroz, F. (2014). Os cemitérios protestantes de Lisboa. *Debater a História*, *5*, 40–48.

Rede de Judiarias de Portugal. (n.d.). *Comunidade Judaica de Belmonte*. https://www.redejudiariasportugal.com/index.php/pt/comunidade-judaica-de-belmonte

Ribeiro, J., & Jorge, B. (2020, May 6). Porto virado a Meca. *JPN-JornalismoPortoNet*. https://www.jpn.up.pt/2020/05/06/porto-virado-a-meca/

RTP Ensina. (2002). *A comunidade hindu em Portugal*. https://ensina.rtp.pt/artigo/a-comunidade-hindu-em-portugal/

Secretariado Nacional da Pastoral da Cultura. (2012). *Catolicismo e outras "Identidades religiosas em Portugal": Todos os resultados do estudo da Universidade Católica*. https://www.snpcultura.org/catolicismo_e_outras_identidades_religiosas_em_portugal.html

Tiesler, N. C. (2000). Muçulmanos na margem: A nova presença Islâmica em Portugal. *Sociologia, Problemas e Práticas*, *34*, 117–144.

Vasconcelos, C. M. (2019, July 21). Para os judeus sefarditas, a terra prometida nunca foi Israel. É Portugal e Espanha. *TSF Rádio Notícias*. https://www.tsf.pt/portugal/sociedade/para-os-judeus-sefarditas-a-terra-prometida-nunca-foi-israel-e-portugal-e-espanha-11120912.html

Xisto, B. O. de O. (2012). *"Assunto encerrado"? Atitudes contemporâneas perante a morte e a cremação em Lisboa* [Master Thesis in Social and Cultural Anthropology]. Universidade de Lisboa.

6 The funeral directing industry

Current structure

In 2019, there were 1,160 funeral homes working in Portugal, employing 3,800 people (Esteves, 2019). The majority of these funeral homes are small family businesses that operate in small areas, in a very traditional way. They are successfully integrated in the community and often have a personal relation with many of the families they serve. Some of the owners represent the third, fourth, or even longer generations in the business. In addition to organizing the funeral, these funeral homes may also assist families with a series of bureaucratic tasks: they may help with the process of inheritance (a process known as *habilitação de herdeiros*) or represent the family in matters related with the sale of graves or tombs.

However, this context has been changing in the 21st century, since Servilusa funeral homes first began to appear in Portugal. Servilusa is the name under which the multinational Mémora group, formed in Spain, has operated in Portugal since 2001. Due to its scale and business model, Servilusa is able to offer innovative and often customized funeral services, which have forced a change of paradigm in this traditional sector. As a result, a progressive shift has been taking place, with traditional family businesses adapting their business model and reinventing themselves to offer similar services as their multinational competitor. According to a report presented by the *APPSF* (*Associação Portuguesa dos Profissionais do Sector Funerário*) in 2011, Servilusa had a 5% market share nationwide (Associação Portuguesa dos Profissionais do Sector Funerário, 2011). In Lisbon, the market share was reported to be 32% in 2006 (Agência LUSA, 2005).

In 2011, the APPSF presented a report that characterized the funeral sector in Portugal and listed some of its biggest limitations,

DOI: 10.4324/9781003153689-6

both at the industry level and at the level of cemetery management. The report referred to topics such as reduced and unqualified staff, neglected environmental issues in the management of cemeteries across the country, overcrowded cemeteries with no available room for expansion, few public funding spent on the construction of new cemeteries, and lack of infrastructure for new facilities, such as crematoria (Associação Portuguesa dos Profissionais do Sector Funerário, 2011).

Associated industries

The funeral sector includes other companies that have as their prime livelihood the supply of materials and accessories for every funeral home across the country. Portuguese coffin manufacturers such as *Joriscastro* are the main suppliers in the Iberian Peninsula (Pinto, 2018); they are located in Amarante, a city in the north of Portugal that is often associated with the production of coffins. *Belartfune* is one of the most popular suppliers for funeral items and religious accessories, as well as *Funerexpress*, a well-known supplier for thanatopraxy and embalming chemicals and other surgical equipment, tools, and refrigerators. Apart from these companies, all the local flower shops near funeral homes meet significant demand for flower displays for the funeral ceremonies, since flowers are still extremely important in the Portuguese funerary tradition. Another relevant sector highly dependent on the funeral directing industry are the stonemason suppliers (which may specialize only in funeral monuments, or supply a variety of other stoneware) and the independent bricklayer professionals, which are mainly local businesses. The role of architects, sculptors, and other academic artists is quite residual in what concerns the conception of monuments, even though it seems to have increased in the last two decades.

Trade fairs and magazines

Since 2016, the funerary sector has organized an annual trade fair, *Expofunerária*, which gathers both national and international companies. There are also multiple trade magazines, such as *Conceito Lutuoso*, *Elegia* (published by the Association of Funeral Directors of Central Portugal [*AAFC*]), and *I-nova* (published by Servilusa), which play a relevant role in announcing and pinpointing some funerary hot topics.

Public perception

The funeral sector in Portugal has often been accused of a lack of transparency. On November 2016, ASAE (*Autoridade de Segurança Alimentar e Económica*, literally Food and Economic Safety Authority) carried out an inspection on funeral homes across Portugal. In this action, which inspected more than 140 funeral homes, ASAE initiated three criminal proceedings relating to price speculation, and ten administrative infraction proceedings for, among other infractions, the lack of pricing and the lack of a catalog of items and services for sale (ASAE, 2016).

The issue of pricing is paramount when it comes to the relationship between funeral homes and consumers. To know the cost of a funeral, for instance, an individual must directly request that information from a specific funeral home and check the price list (which is mandatory by law and technically public, but not easily accessible). This means, in practice, that most consumers are not aware of any pricing information until they find themselves in a position where they must quickly organize a funeral. A survey conducted by DECO (*Associação Portuguesa para a Defesa do Consumidor*, Portuguese Association for Consumer Protection) in 2008 concluded that 20% of all funerals held in Portugal turned out to be more expensive than expected. Of the 20% of families who requested to know the funeral cost beforehand, 60% did not receive any kind of budget or price forecast in advance. Another important finding from this study is that the overwhelming majority of families only contact one funeral home before making decisions for the funeral ("DECO Ajuda a Lidar Com as Agências Funerárias," 2008). An earlier study, also conducted by DECO in 2002, had already drawn attention to the lack of transparency in the funeral sector. According to the 2002 study, 67% of agencies did not indicate the price of a coffin upon request, 45% gave little information about funeral accessories, 36% provided little information about the overall service, and 34% did show the coffin at all prior to the purchase ("Funerárias Contestadas," 2002).

This lack of transparency had already been alluded to in the introductory text of Decreto-Lei n.° 206/2001, the first legal document (now revoked) that attempted to regulate the funeral sector. According to the introductory text, 'the activity of funeral homes has been marked, over the last few years, by the increase in less transparent situations, which cannot but be a cause for concern, as this is an activity with significant social relevance.'

The work of the funeral director

The work of a funeral director in Portugal consists of carrying out all tasks related to the stages before, during, and after the funeral, including transporting the corpse, cleaning and dressing, scheduling the cemetery and funeral ceremonies, and, finally, filing in all the paperwork related with post-mortem legal issues that need to be addressed.

There is a general perception that the funeral sector in Portugal is dominated by men, with few women working in it (Fernando Oliveira and António Matos, personal communications). There are no specific surveys performed on the subject, and studies on the funeral sector in general are rare, but many seem to support the hypothesis that the sector is male-dominated. A case study carried out with a family-owned funeral home in 2012 sought to explore, among other variables, the gender relations at play. The study found that of the four family members and four hired staff involved in the company, only one was a woman. The agency specifically stated their intent to hire more women (Santos, 2012). Another study, conducted with 60 funeral professionals working at Servilusa had a sample composed of 70% men and 30% women (Cabo, 2014). This hypothesis may also apply to cemetery staff: a study on the emotions of Portuguese gravediggers regarding death had an all-male sample (Zelenovic, 2008). In the press, cases of female gravediggers are often presented as rare or curious (Ferreira, 2021; Julião, 2010; Rodrigues, 2020).

Embalming and thanatopraxy

Embalming (*embalsamamento*) and thanatopraxy (*tanatopraxia*) procedures consist of a temporary form of preservation of the corpse. In Portugal, embalming is the term most often used in relation to preparation of corpses for repatriation; conversely, thanatopraxy is the term most often used in relation to the preparation of corpses for funeral viewings (Miranda, 2016). Although, strictly speaking, thanatopraxy may be thought of as a form of embalming, the two concepts differ. Embalming can be performed by funeral directors or by operatives at the National Institute of Legal Medicine and Forensic Sciences (INMLCF). It emphasizes the preservation of the body for a longer period of time, in order to allow repatriation, and may have the consequence of worsening the aesthetic appearance of the corpse. Conversely, thanatopraxy is a procedure exclusive to the funeral sector, and its purpose is that of maintaining the natural appearance of the body after death.

Thanatopraxy was first legalized in 2010, with Decree-Law 109/2010, and regulated in 2015, with *Portaria* 162-A/2015.

Because, in Portugal, the legal deadline for burying or cremating a body is 72 hours, temporary preservation procedures are not considered necessary for the vast majority of wakes. Therefore, thanatopraxy is applied only at the request of families. It is an expensive procedure, costing 850 euros in 2016, and it is provided by multinational company Servilusa in around 95% of cases (Miranda, 2016).

Table 6.1 indicates an increase in the number and proportion of thanatopraxy procedures between 2010 and 2016.

While, in other European countries, most temporary preservation procedures are carried out for repatriations, in Portugal, the opposite happens. In 2015, 2,078 thanatopraxy services were performed by Servilusa alone, which contrasts with the 30 embalmings carried out per year at the INMLCF (Miranda, 2016).

In 2016, there were only eight certified embalmers in Portugal, all of whom had been trained and certified abroad by the French Institute of Thanatopraxy. This European certification allows these professionals to work as independent providers of thanatopraxy services. Conversely, national certification only allows professionals to perform thanatopraxy as staff members of a funeral home. The national certification in thanatopraxy may be obtained after attending and passing a 50-hour training module (officially referred to as a Unidade de Formação de Curta Duração, meaning Short-Term Training Unit, abbreviated as UFCD) in thanatopraxy. As it is currently offered, this training module is purely theoretical and does not provide any

Table 6.1 Evolution of number of thanatopraxy procedures, 2010–2016

Year	Total number of thanatopraxy procedures	Total number of deaths	Thanatopraxy procedures per total number of deaths (percentage)
2010	241	105,954	0.23
2011	930	102,848	0.90
2012	911	107,612	0.85
2013	1,058	106,554	0.99
2014	1,140	104,843	1.09
2015	2,078	108,539	1.91
2016	1,250	110,573	1.13

Sources: Based on FFMS – Fundação Francisco Manuel dos Santos. (2020). Óbitos de residentes em Portugal: Total e no primeiro ano de vida; Miranda, A. J. de A. (2016). Thanatopraxy in Portugal: Modern embalming genesis and its forensic applications by a medicolegal viewpoint.

practical preparation for thanatopraxy and embalming procedures. The module may be taken alone or as part of the national professional course for funeral directors, but many of the funeral directors who attend the course end up never taking this module, as there is no availability on the part of certified embalmers to provide the training. This unavailability stems from the fact that most of the certified embalmers in Portugal work for Servilusa and may not provide training outside the company (Miguel Moreira, personal communication).

Since 2018, Instituto CRIAP, a private training institution, has included in its training offer a thanatopraxy and embalming specialization, with practical modules on corpses, for funeral directors and any professionals in the field that want to pursue this career. This could potentially increase the number of registered professionals in the embalming field (assuming those professionals are integrated in funeral homes and begin to offer embalming and thanatopraxy services, otherwise they are not obliged to be registered), but to this day, we have no knowledge that there's been an increase in the registration of new embalmers or funeral homes in the Northern region, offering embalming or thanatopraxy services (Miguel Moreira, personal communication).

References

Agência LUSA. (2005, August 3). *Servilusa investe 2ME para expandir actividade no Norte*. https://www.rtp.pt/noticias/economia/servilusa-investe-2me-para-expandir-actividade-no-norte_n75953

ASAE. (2016, December). *Agências Funerárias—Atividade Operacional*. https://www.asae.gov.pt/newsletter2/asaenews-n-104-dezembro-2016/agencias-funerarias.aspx

Associação Portuguesa dos Profissionais do Sector Funerário. (2011, January). *Caracterização do Mercado Português*. https://app.parlamento.pt/webutils/docs/doc.pdf?path=6148523063446f764c324679626d-56304c334e706447567a4c31684a5447566e6e4c304e5054543338325130464653555765235152425269394562324e31625756756447397a51574e3061585a705a4746b5a554e7662576c7a6536332463764c7a44268a4459775954466d4c5c5455324d44445744e474e69596931684e6d49794794c57466d5a6d566d4f4f47526a597a59344e43357575a47593d6fich=0a860a1f-5601-4cbb-a6b2-affef8dcc684.pdf&Inline=true

Cabo, L. J. L. de M. (2014). *Ansiedade em face da morte em Agentes Funerários* [Master Thesis in Clinical Psychology]. Instituto Superior Miguel Torga - Escola Superior de Altos Estudos (ESAE).

DECO Ajuda a Lidar Com as Agências Funerárias. (2008, October 31). *TVI 24*. https://tvi24.iol.pt/sociedade/funerais/deco-ajuda-a-lidar-com-as-agencias-funerarias

Esteves, C. (2019, October 26). A última conta: O negócio dos funerais. *Expresso*. https://expresso.pt/sociedade/2019-10-26-A-ultima-conta-o-negocio-dos-funerais

Ferreira, M. L. (2021, February 18). Miguel, Fausto, Ricardo e Diana: A vida dos coveiros do Alto de São João, no fim da linha da Covid-19. *Observador*. https://observador.pt/especiais/miguel-fausto-ricardo-e-diana-a-vida-dos-coveiros-do-alto-de-sao-joao-no-fim-da-linha-da-covid-19/

FFMS - Fundação Francisco Manuel dos Santos. (2020). *Óbitos de residentes em Portugal: Total e no primeiro ano de vida*. PORDATA - Base de Dados de Portugal Contemporâneo. https://www.pordata.pt/Portugal/%c3%93bitos+de+residentes+em+Portugal+total+e+no+primeiro+ano+de+vida-15

Funerárias Contestadas. (2002, October 30). *CM Jornal*. https://www.cmjornal.pt/portugal/detalhe/funerarias-contestadas

Julião, P. (2010, November 1). Maria "Coveira" enterra os mortos como há meio século. *Diário de Notícias*. https://www.dn.pt/portugal/maria-coveira-enterra-os-mortos-como-ha-meio-seculo-1700163.html

Miranda, A. J. de A. (2016). *Thanatopraxy in Portugal: Modern Embalming Genesis and Its Forensic Applications by a Medicolegal Viewpoint* [Master Thesis in Forensic Medicine, Instituto de Ciências Biomédicas Abel Salazar da Universidade do Porto]. https://sigarra.up.pt/icbas/pt/pub_geral.pub_view?pi_pub_base_id=175381

Pinto, B. S. (2018, November 1). Os milhões do negócio da morte. *Sábado*. https://www.sabado.pt/dinheiro/detalhe/os-milhoes-do-negocio-da-morte

Santos, J. J. dos. (2012). *Trabalhar com a Morte e Gerir o Trabalho em Família—Estudo de Caso numa Agência Funerária* [Master Thesis in Psychology]. Universidade Católica Portuguesa.

Zelenovic, C. C. C. M. (2008). *Representações e emoções de coveiros portugueses face à morte* [Master Thesis in Psychology]. Universidade Fernando Pessoa.

7   A typical funeral

It is estimated that 80%–90% of Portuguese funerals are conducted according to the principles of the Catholic Church ("Funerais Laicos Ainda São Uma Minoria," 2010). For that reason, this chapter describes a typical Catholic funeral. The Catholic funeral typically practiced in Portugal is divided into three consecutive parts, or stations (*estações*): the wake, the funeral mass, and the rite of committal. The liturgical norms associated with each station are presented in *Celebração das Exéquias (Conferência Episcopal Portuguesa, 2020)*, the manual that explains the Order of Christian Funerals according to The Roman Ritual.

All three stations are public events, available for anyone who wants to attend. For this reason, it is common for funeral homes to post obituaries on the windows of local shops (e.g. pharmacies, florists), chapels, and the funeral home itself. These obituaries may also be published in local newspapers or posted online. Usually, the obituary announces the location and starting time of the wake, the location and starting time of the funeral mass, and the location of the cemetery or crematorium where the body will be committed once the funeral has ended. The process is relatively quick: it is common to begin the wake on the day of the death and to bury the body the following day. This is consistent with Portuguese funerary law, which establishes that bodies must be buried within 24–72 hours after death.

Funerals in Portugal do not vary greatly across the country; nor have they changed significantly over the years (Fernando Oliveira, personal communication). One main shift has been observed in recent years, which has created a differentiation between rural and urban areas: this has to do with the location of the wake. Traditionally, the three stations of the funeral would take place in different locations, with the wake taking place in the home of the deceased, the funeral in the local church, and the rite of committal in the cemetery. Additionally, there would be two processions: the first from the home

DOI: 10.4324/9781003153689-7

of the deceased to the church, and the second from the church to the cemetery. This setup may still be seen in some rural areas today, but it has become rare in urban areas, where the wake is more likely to take place in a public location. If this location is close to the location of the funeral (or indeed, the same), the first procession may be suppressed.

The wake

A typical Portuguese funeral starts with the wake (*velório*). During the wake, the dead body is displayed in the coffin for a period of around 24 hours. Open-coffin wakes are the norm, but closed-coffin wakes are permitted. The tradition used to be to hold the wake in the home of the deceased, but now it has become common practice to hold it in a public place, such as a mortuary home (*casa mortuária*, a building specifically prepared for this purpose and managed by a local authority, Catholic brotherhood, or private entity), a local chapel or church (provided it can be occupied for the duration of the wake), or a funerary center.

Funeral home staff transport the body of the deceased to the location of the wake in a hearse. Embalming is not standard practice in Portugal, and neither are post-mortem cosmetic procedures such as makeup; generally, the body undergoes minimal preparation in order to improve its appearance prior to the wake. The eyes are closed, the hair combed, and the body is dressed in formal or semiformal clothing and footwear, which has been previously provided by the family to funeral home staff. Because this preparation work is so minimal, it is often done in the hospital morgue (since most deaths occur in-hospital); then, the body is transported directly to the wake. In case embalming and more in-depth preparation work is required, then the funeral home transports the body from the hospital to their premises first, and then to the wake.

If the wake is to take place in a chapel or church, the coffin is placed on a bier before the altar, usually perpendicular to it, as if the deceased were facing the altar. Coffins tend to be of simple design (types of coffin are discussed in-depth in Chapter 9), but they are not presented unadorned during the wake; usually, there is a textile layer under the body, and a textile layer over the body. The underlayer may be part of the coffin or added on by the funeral home; it may be simple (e.g. a white cotton or linen sheet) or elaborate (e.g. made from lace, satin, or velvet, with decorative trimmings). This underlayer also includes a pillow to elevate the head of the deceased. The textile overlayer also varies in appearance: it may be present as a small square of cloth (to cover the face of the deceased), a large sheet (to cover the body, partially or completely, if so desired by the family), or a see-through veil (to cover the face without obscuring it completely). All these options may be made from simple white cloth, or printed, embroidered, and trimmed with various religious motifs.

The coffin is often surrounded by candles on floor stands (usually called *tocheiros*, literally 'torchers'), usually four, one placed at each corner of the coffin. A cup of holy water is placed at the foot of the deceased, so that visitors can sprinkle the body upon arrival. These objects may be provided by the funeral home, or by the administration of the location where the wake is taking place.

This initial setup may also include a small number of floral arrangements, usually paid for by the family upon arranging the funeral. These first arrangements are usually placed on tripod stands. Specific floral arrangements are used in funerals: wreaths (referred to as *coroas*, or 'crowns,' ring-shaped floral arrangements with a typical diameter of 60–90 cm) and sprays (*palmas*, large, flat bouquets).

Finally, the setup is completed by a condolence book, usually sitting on a pedestal by the entrance to the room. These items are provided by the funeral home, at a cost, with the understanding that the book is later delivered to the family. This same pedestal may also carry small prayer cards with some basic information on the deceased (name, birth and death dates, and a photograph) and a suggested prayer. These cards are also provided by the funeral home at a cost, and visitors are expected to carry them home.

A priest may preside over the wake, but this is not always the case. In fact, most wakes are unstructured events, developing as a series of informal, small-scale interactions between mourners. It is rare that any person will address others as an audience, and so eulogies are extremely uncommon. Close family members tend to sit toward the front of the room, closer to the body of the deceased. When other visitors arrive at the wake, they begin by offering their condolences to this group and paying their respects to the body of the deceased (by sprinkling it with holy water or offering a prayer). Most visitors also bring flowers for the deceased. They may bring *coroas* or *palmas*, but it is also not frowned upon for visitors to bring smaller bouquets or even homegrown flowers. If the deceased was a member of any association or group, then it is common for the association to collectively purchase

Figure 7.1 Cups with holy water at the feet of recent perpetual graves in Out-
eiro (municipality of Viana do Castelo).

Note: The use of holy water is still very popular in some rural cemeteries of northern
Portugal. In some, the cups can be found at the entrance of the cemetery itself, as in a
Catholic church.

a *coroa* or *palma*. Flowers are not typically handed to family members, but instead placed directly on or around the coffin. Visitors may
leave shortly after this initial contact with the family, or take a seat
elsewhere in the room to pray, chat with other visitors, or simply sit
in silence. Typically, close family and close friends tend to stay longer,

and some may even choose to stay with the body overnight, although this practice is no longer as widespread as it used to be.

Funeral home staff may be present for the entirety of the wake, or simply check in periodically to assist the family on any practical matters that may arise. Most wakes have minimal intervention from funeral home staff, but others may be more 'managed,' including, for instance, refreshments such as water, tea, and coffee, depending on whether the location allows for it. Chapels or churches will typically not allow it, while funerary centers will be prepared for it.

The funeral mass

The funeral mass is conducted by a priest, in a chapel or church, with the body of the deceased positioned in the church as if facing the altar. If the wake has already taken place in a chapel or church, the body need not be moved between the two stations. If not, the body may need to be moved. This may be done, depending on the distance: by hand by pallbearers, on a wheeled bier, on a hand-drawn hearse, or in a hearse car. Depending on local custom, the start of the funeral mass may be announced by church bells. In many places, there is a specific way of tolling the bells: first to announce death, with the number of last tolls indicating whether the deceased was male or female, and then to announce burial. This last tolling can be, in some cases, longer or more intense.

Unlike the wake, the funeral mass is highly formulaic, following a strict structure laid out in *Celebração das Exéquias*. The funeral mass is one type of mass among many, including many familiar elements from a typical mass, such as prayers, hymns, readings, and even Holy Communion. For this reason, opportunities for families to participate in and customize the ceremony are limited. Although the funeral mass mentions the deceased by name, and families may request specific Bible readings, or specific hymns, they may not deviate from a set of pre-approved options. Family members may do the readings themselves, but eulogies are once again not encouraged, and the use of recorded videos or slideshows is also explicitly discouraged (Conferência Episcopal Portuguesa, 2020, p. 104). The priest may offer a brief homily, but it may not take the form or style of an eulogy. Typically, a funeral mass will last around one and a half hours.

Wakes and funerals are attended, first and foremost, by family members of the deceased; friends, colleagues, and acquaintances make up the rest of the attendance. The elderly make up a significant part of the attendees; conversely, teenagers and children will rarely attend funerals, unless the deceased was a close family member or friend. It is not possible to pinpoint a typical number of attendants, since the number will vary drastically depending on factors such as the profession of the deceased (or of close family members), membership in any associations, notoriety in the community, and social status. The wider the person's social circle, the more people will typically attend the funeral. If the deceased has met an untimely, unexpected, or violent death, this will also result in greater attendance. It is important to consider that, while most Portuguese funerals are Catholic, the attendees may not necessarily be involved in regular Catholic practice; as such, it is increasingly common to see funeral attendees who behave in accordance with the solemnity of the occasion (e.g. standing and sitting when required), but who do not actively participate in prayers or hymns, and who opt out of receiving Holy Communion.

Black is the traditional color of mourning, and it used to be tradition to wear black and formal or semiformal clothing to funerals. As wakes and funerals have become more informal over the years, it is now common to attend in everyday clothes, provided that they are subdued enough for the religious context. Likewise, the custom to wear black for a period of mourning after a funeral is no longer common. Elderly widows may still choose to wear black for life, but the custom is now considered to be old-fashioned.

The rite of committal

The rite of committal consists of a very short prayer conducted by the priest, lasting only a few minutes. Although it is meant to take place at the place of committal—the cemetery or crematorium—the rite of committal may also take place in the church, in cases where the priest does not accompany the body to the place of committal. This may happen because of overlapping commitments on the part of the priest, or because the cemetery is too distant from the church. In most cases, however, the priest will accompany the body.

As the funeral mass comes to an end, the coffin is closed, and the funeral home staff prepare to transport the coffin to the cemetery. Depending on the distance, this may be done by hand by pallbearers, on a wheeled bier, on a hand-drawn hearse, or in a hearse car. Portuguese hearse cars are similar to transport vans; usually, they have room for the coffin and floral arrangements in the back, and for a few mourners, usually close family, in the backseat. The back portion of the hearse is all made from glass, so that the coffin is always visible to those following the hearse to the cemetery. The priest and mourners tend to follow either by foot or by car. This part of the funeral is referred to as *cortejo fúnebre*, or funeral procession, and is accompanied by prayers or hymns, led by the priest.

Figure 7.2 A hand-drawn hearse at the local cemetery of Esgueira, Aveiro.

Upon arrival, the body is transported into the cemetery by hand, on a wheeled bier, or on a hand-drawn hearse. Family members often ask to carry the coffin, but they will not typically carry it directly to the open grave. Instead, they will set it down on a bier on the path that is immediately adjacent to the grave. This is where the priest will usually perform the rite of committal. As stated earlier, this is a short prayer, usually lasting less than five minutes.

Once the rite of committal has been made, cemetery staff carry the coffin to the open grave. There, they use a system of straps to gradually lower the coffin into the grave. The grave is immediately backfilled, usually using shovels; in most cases, there is no machinery involved. Once the grave has been covered, cemetery staff place the floral arrangements from the wake and funeral on top of it.

There is no set moment for mourners to leave the cemetery. While some may leave immediately after the rite of committal, others will wait until the coffin has been lowered into the grave. Others may wait longer still, until the grave has been fully backfilled. Mourners will generally disperse after this point, as there is no social obligation for families to provide a meal after the funeral, or for other people to provide the family with a meal.

Figure 7.3 Floral arrangements on a recently filled grave.

Variations related to cremation

The *Celebração das Exéquias* has accounted for funerals with cremation since 2006. In such cases, the wake and funeral can also be performed, as described here, without major differences. The main difference will have to do with the rite of committal, which is usually performed at the gravesite; with cremation, it may take place in the church, before the body is transported to the crematorium, or at the crematorium, provided that the priest accompanies the body.

According to the Catholic Church, ashes should be buried or entombed in the cemetery, rather than scattered or kept in the home. However, research suggests that families who resort to priests for Catholic funeral masses do not usually provide information or seek counsel regarding the intended fate of the ashes. They may disperse or bury the ashes outside the cemetery, essentially disregarding Catholic doctrine on this part of the process (Xisto, 2012). This is consistent with the general behavior of the Portuguese regarding funerals, in the sense that they rely on the Catholic Church for the wake and funeral rituals (and may follow them with another mass seven days later), but do not necessarily seek to prolong their adherence to the precepts of the Church beyond that point.

The Seventh Day Mass

Generally, mourners will congregate for another mass seven days after the funeral mass. Known as *Missa do Sétimo Dia* (literally, Seventh Day Mass), this mass is also a highly structured mass that mentions the deceased by name, but does not dwell on details of their life. This mass is generally less crowded than the funeral mass, but it is no less important, as it creates a second opportunity to participate in funeral rites. This can be particularly convenient for distant family members, for example, who may not have been able to attend the funeral mass. During the period between the funeral and the *Missa do Sétimo Dia*, many funeral homes will also publish, on newspapers or their online channels, a thank you note on behalf of the family. This is usually a standard message thanking all who have attended the wake and funeral. It is not expected that families will thank mourners individually. Families who are more actively Catholic may also request masses 30 days after the funeral mass, or on the deceased person's birthday.

References

Conferência Episcopal Portuguesa. (2020). *Celebração das Exéquias*. Secretariado Nacional de Liturgia.

Funerais laicos ainda são uma minoria. (2010, November 1). *Público*. https://www.publico.pt/2010/11/01/jornal/funerais-laicos-ainda-sao-uma-minoria-20525520

Xisto, B. O. de O. (2012). *"Assunto encerrado"? Atitudes contemporâneas perante a morte e a cremação em Lisboa* [Master Thesis in Social and Cultural Anthropology]. Universidade de Lisboa.

8   Paying for funerals

The costs of a funeral service depend on a variety of factors. The geographic location can be influential in the sense that, in urban areas, there may be greater purchasing power, which may in turn motivate funeral homes to offer more expensive services with extra features and add-ons; on the other hand, urban areas may have a greater number of funeral homes, which may lead to more competitive pricing. The service will also influence the final costs: for instance, funerals with cremation may offer an opportunity to save on the coffin, which tends to be simpler, but may also create extra expenses with transportation if the crematorium is too distant.

The total cost of a funeral is listed by the funeral home on a detailed invoice, which usually includes: the coffin and respective textiles, the outfit of the deceased (in cases where the family has not provided one), the transportation of the body, the cost of floral arrangements and prayer cards, and rental fees for materials needed for the funeral (e.g. textiles, carpets, candles, chairs). The funeral home will also charge an administrative fee for handling bureaucracy related to the person's death. External fees may also feature in this invoice if handled by the funeral home; however, they ultimately revert back to the provider. These external fees may include burial or cremation fees (see below), or fees paid to the priest for the religious ceremony. The cost of a funeral mass is 30 euros across multiple dioceses. Other masses, which families may choose to request later, cost ten euros (*Tabela de Taxas e Tributos*, 2008).

Although the funeral includes so many elements, it is possible to find funeral services that cost around 990 euros. This amount may seem arbitrary, but it allows agencies to charge for their service and still leave some room for external expenses, thus allowing the consumer to pay around 1,316.43 euros in total. This is the amount the state will reimburse for funeral expenses. This could be considered an affordable funeral, and it is only slightly lower than what the

DOI: 10.4324/9781003153689-8

press often reports as being average: between 1,500 and 1,700 euros ("Preços Cobrados Vão de 33 a 250 Euros Por Cada Cremação," 2008).

On the higher end of the spectrum, a funeral service costing 3,000 euros could be considered expensive. There is no upper limit to how expensive a funeral can be, though. Funeral homes offer so many services that a family could easily spend thousands of euros on the coffin alone (coffins made from exotic woods like *pau preto*, for example, are among the most expensive). Thanatopraxy, musical tributes, and custom options for ash disposal, such as diamonds made from cremation ashes, can also add up to create truly extravagant funerals.

The market for prepaid funerals is growing in Portugal. According to the funeral sector, prepaid funerals allow individuals to retain control over their own funeral, or to save their living relatives the burden of having to handle it themselves. One of the main providers of this type of service, Servilusa, refers to prepaid funerals as 'Plano Funeral em Vida'. Servilusa arranges an average of 100 prepaid funeral contracts per year (Queiroz, 2020). Customers of the 'Plano Funeral em Vida' are promised that the entire ceremony, down to the smallest details, will be conducted according to their wishes. There is also an element of financial savings involved, as the plan promises to sell a future service at today's price; that is, it promises to protect the client from inflation. Payment can be single or in several instalments without interest, and the contracted services can be modified at any time.

State assistance for funeral expenses

The minimum wage in Portugal was set at 665 euros per month for 2021. Considering that 25.6% of Portuguese workers are earning the minimum wage (Gabinete de Estratégia e Planeamento, 2021), even the most affordable funeral can be considered to be a significant expense. The Portuguese government offers two options to alleviate funeral costs: a reimbursement of funeral expenses (*reembolso das despesas de funeral*) and a funeral subsidy (*subsídio de funeral*).

Access to the reimbursement of funeral expenses is dependent on the deceased having contributed to the Social Security system through taxes throughout their working life. In such cases, the individual who pays for the funeral service becomes eligible to claim a refund, which is of 1,316.43 euros. In cases where the deceased did not contribute to Social Security through taxes, the person paying the funeral is still entitled to a funeral subsidy from the state, of 219.96 euros. It is important to mention that, in Portugal, all employed individuals are automatically enrolled in the Social Security system. While some exemptions are possible, the vast majority of Portuguese citizens have contributed to the Social Security system throughout their life and, therefore, qualify for the higher value option, the reimbursement of funeral expenses.

Regardless of who pays for the funeral service, the government ensures a monthly widowhood pension paid to the living spouse that can reach up to 60% of the deceased's salary. The same reality is applied to the orphan's pension (for children of the deceased person).

A third option that helps citizens overcome financial limitations in regards to funeral expenses is the welfare funeral (*funeral social*). The welfare funeral is a legal right of every citizen who requests it, and any funeral home or IPSS is legally obliged to provide it and cannot charge more than the sum defined by law—which as of the 2020 update was 412 euros (Direção-Geral das Atividades Económicas, 2020). The burial fee charged by the cemetery is not included in this value, but most cemeteries will waive it regardless. This funeral option is also available for the disposal of unclaimed bodies in Portuguese morgues, but it is common for both funeral homes and cemeteries to waive fees in those cases.

Portaria 1237-A/2010 defines the essential components that make up a welfare funeral. The service must include a pine wood coffin or equivalent, equipped with hardware and textiles. It must include individual funeral transport, and all the technical services necessary for the funeral, which ought to be provided by the agency. Through these components, we understand what the Portuguese law considers to be a dignified funeral.

The cost of burial

In Portugal, the cost of burial is made up of two elements: the burial or entombment fee (which pays for the act of physically placing the body in the grave or tomb) and the concession fee (which pays for the right to keep a person buried in perpetuity in the cemetery, in a grave or tomb). Families who choose to bury their loved one in a temporary grave need not pay the latter. The cost of these fees varies significantly from cemetery to cemetery. In order to illustrate this variation, we have collected data from 14 Portuguese cemeteries: Table 8.1 shows the cost of burial and entombment fees and the cost of perpetual concession fees for graves and private tombs.

Table 8.1 Fees in selected Portuguese cemeteries, by region, in euros (rounded)

Region	Cemeteries	Burial fee		Entombment fee	Perpetual concession fees	
		Temporary grave	Perpetual grave	Private tomb	Grave (per individual grave)	Private tomb (per m^2)
Northern Portugal	Bragança municipal	37	55	29	317	194
	Porto municipal	46	107	107	2,122	826
Central Portugal	Coimbra municipal	51	95	76	2,280	950
	Esgueira local	70	70	50	1,100	1,000
Lisbon Region	Lisbon municipal	87	150	195	9,996	1,666
	Sintra municipal	65	100	113	3,023	1,574
Alentejo	Elvas municipal	40	n/a	90	980	300
	Évora municipal	63	94	61	929	470
Algarve	Faro municipal cemeteries	14	58	18	725	435
	Aljezur municipal cemeteries	108	108	37	761	746
Azores	Angra do Heroísmo municipal cemeteries	30	66	60	1,000	500
	Ponta Delgada municipal cemeteries	10	49	121	484	193
Madeira	Porto Moniz municipal cemeteries	35	50	40	400	417
	Funchal municipal cemeteries	107	n/a	197	n/a	1,407

Sources: Câmara Municipal de Aljezur (2015); Câmara Municipal de Angra do Heroísmo (2014); Câmara Municipal de Bragança (2020); Câmara Municipal de Coimbra (2017); Câmara Municipal de Elvas (2019); Câmara Municipal de Évora (2021); Câmara Municipal de Faro (n.d.); Câmara Municipal de Lisboa (2020); Câmara Municipal de Ponta Delgada (2020); Câmara Municipal de Sintra (2018); Câmara Municipal do Funchal (2019); Câmara Municipal do Porto (2021); Câmara Municipal do Porto Moniz (2010); Junta de Freguesia de Esgueira (2015).

By the general overview of Table 8.1, we can conclude that the most expensive burial fees are found in the Lisbon Region, followed by Northern Portugal, Algarve, and Madeira. The most expensive fees for burial in temporary graves come from the Funchal municipal cemeteries, followed by the Aljezur and Lisbon municipal cemeteries. A distinct situation happens when analyzing burial fees in perpetual graves, with the Oporto municipal cemeteries jumping to the top of the list. Finally, entombment fees in private tombs are higher in the Funchal and Lisbon municipal cemeteries. Regarding the cheapest options, Ponta Delgada cemetery, in the Azores, bears the cheapest fees for burial in temporary as well as perpetual graves. Finally, Faro has the cheapest fee for entombment in private tombs.

Regarding concessions for graves and tombs, according to Table 8.1, the most expensive options for the concession of perpetual graves are found in Lisbon, Coimbra, and Sintra, while for tombs, Lisbon, Sintra, and Funchal cemeteries bear the highest concession cost per square meter. In line with the previous table, Ponta Delgada and Bragança cemeteries have the cheapest concession fees for both perpetual graves and tombs.

There are many reasons why some cemeteries may be cheaper than others. Practical reasons, such as the availability of burial space, play a part in how expensive burial can be; we see this in the tendency for fees and concession values to be higher in the most populated regions of the country. To put it into perspective, the cost of a perpetual grave concession in Lisbon, at 9,996 euros, is higher than the annual salary of a minimum wage worker. Conversely, these areas are also where the purchasing power of the population is generally higher. Public cemeteries in poorer areas will necessarily have to adapt their fees to the purchasing power of the population. There is also another factor which cannot be discounted, which is the influence that each executive board has in the management of public cemeteries. Since prices are not guided by the state, and cemeteries represent a valuable source of revenue for municipalities and civil parishes, executive boards have considerable leeway to make decisions regarding costs.

When it comes to comparing the costs of burial in a temporary grave and in a perpetual grave, it would be simplistic to look at burial fees alone. It is also important to consider the cost of each option over time. In the short term, burial in a temporary grave is more affordable, and this can be appealing at a time when families are burdened by funeral expenses. However, when families pay for burial in a temporary grave, they are effectively committing themselves to additional expenses in the long term. The body will have to be exhumed, and arrangements will have to be made regarding the destination of the skeletal remains. Families who decide to keep the remains in the cemetery will have to purchase a concession for an ossuary niche and buy an ossuary urn, at minimum. Families who decide to cremate the remains will incur similar expenses if they decide to keep the ashes in the cemetery, besides having to pay for the cremation itself.

Families who opt for burial in a perpetual grave will initially spend more on the burial fee and the concession itself. They will also incur expenses with the construction of the monument, and then with its maintenance. The simplest of grave monuments may cost around 500 euros, with mid-range models falling around the 1,500 euros to 2,000 euros range (we discuss the process of acquiring a monument in detail in Chapter 11). However, these families will not have to pay for exhumations in the future (unless they specifically request them), and they will not have to purchase further concessions to keep skeletal remains or ashes in the cemetery. This is especially true in the case of family tombs, since these spaces can accommodate not only multiple coffins, but also ossuary urns and cremation urns.

These nuances are going to be relevant in cemeteries where burial space is still widely available, and where families may still, therefore, be able to choose between temporary or perpetual graves. In cemeteries where a shortage of burial space is the norm, however, the cost of a perpetual concession will be too steep for most families to even consider it as a viable option. We can see these two cases clearly in the data presented in this chapter: in the Bragança municipal cemeteries, the cost of a perpetual burial right is around eight times larger than the burial fee in a temporary grave; in the Lisbon municipal cemeteries, it is over 100 times larger.

The cost of cremation

Cremation is generally considered to be an affordable alternative to burial. This may stem from the idea that, with cremation, coffins are cheaper and there are no extra expenses associated with the construction and maintenance of monuments. However, this does not necessarily mean that cremation itself is cheap. We can draw a direct comparison in public cemeteries that also manage crematoria. In the Lisbon municipal cemeteries, cremation costs 152.85 euros while burial in a temporary grave costs 87.45 euros (Câmara Municipal de

Lisboa, 2020). In the Oporto municipal cemeteries, cremation costs a minimum of 84.16 euros while burial in a temporary grave costs 46.39 euros (Câmara Municipal do Porto, 2021). In both cases, the more affordable form of cremation is no longer more affordable than the most affordable form of burial.

There are also other fees involved when families choose cremation, and especially when they choose to keep the ashes in the cemetery. In these cases, forms of non-individualized disposal (remembrance gardens and cremation deposits) are more affordable than placement in a columbarium, in an individual niche. In the Lisbon municipal cemeteries, for example, cremation costs 152.85 euros. Pouring the ashes in a cendrarium (or cremation deposit) would cost the family a one-time fee of 52.50 euros. However, placing them in a columbarium niche would cost a fee of 193.85 euros every five years (Câmara Municipal de Lisboa, 2020). In the Oporto municipal cemeteries, the placement of the ashes in the rose garden is included with the cremation fee (which, as mentioned, costs 84.16 euros). However, if a family wished to place the ashes in an individual niche, they would pay a higher cremation fee of 125.65 euros. Then, they would pay a yearly fee of 36.08 euros in order to maintain the use of the niche. If they failed to pay the fee, the ashes would be considered abandoned and would be ultimately removed (Câmara Municipal do Porto, 2021).

As more and more people opt for cremation, the phenomenon of cemetery overcrowding may transfer into one of columbarium overcrowding. The Lisbon and Oporto municipal cemeteries provide an example of a new reality, where many public cemeteries no longer offer perpetual concessions for columbaria, instead charging for a renewable lease. Variation across the country is still low, with yearly fees for columbaria in many cemeteries costing an average of 30–40 euros.

References

Câmara Municipal de Aljezur. (2015). *Regulamento Geral de Taxas e Licenças do Município de Aljezur*. https://cms.cm-aljezur.pt//upload_files/client_id_2/website_id_1/Atividade_Municipal/Regulamentos/29-Regulamento%20Geral%20de%20Taxas%20e%20Licencas%20do%20Municipio%20de%20Aljezur.pdf

Câmara Municipal de Angra do Heroísmo. (2014). *Tabela Municipal de Taxas de Angra do Heroísmo*. http://angradoheroismo.pt/wp-content/uploads/2019/02/13.pdf

Câmara Municipal de Bragança. (2020). *Tabela de Taxas para 2020*. https://www.cm-braganca.pt/cmbraganca2020/uploads/document/file/3949/tabela_de_taxas_2020.pdf

Câmara Municipal de Coimbra. (2017). *Tabela Geral de Taxas Municipais.* https://www.cm-coimbra.pt/wp-content/uploads/2017/07/53.%20Edital%20 53_2017.pdf

Câmara Municipal de Elvas. (2019). *Regulamento Geral de Taxas Municipais e Tabela de Taxas – 2019.* https://www.cm-elvas.pt/wp-content/ uploads/2020/08/Reg.Taxas-2019.pdf

Câmara Municipal de Évora. (2021). *Regulamento e Tabela de Taxas e Outras Receitas do Município de Évora 2021.* http://arquivo2020.cm-evora. pt/pt/site-municipio/atividademunicipio/Regulamentos/Documents/ RTTORME%202021_%28vers%c3%a3o%201_2021%29.pdf

Câmara Municipal de Faro. (n.d.). *Tabela de Taxas Gerais do Município de Faro 2018.* https://cms.cm-faro.pt//upload_files/client_id_1/website_ id_1/EDITAIS%20E%20AVISOS/Tabela%20de%20taxas%20gerais%20 2018_VF.pdf

Câmara Municipal de Lisboa. (2020). *Tabela de Taxas Municipais 2021.* https://www.lisboa.pt/fileadmin/download_center/normativas/taxas_ precos/TTM_BM_1402_4sup_Deliberacao_384_Proposta_791_30_ dez_2020.pdf

Câmara Municipal de Ponta Delgada. (2020). *Tabela de Taxas e Licenças 2021.* https://www.cm-pontadelgada.pt/cmpontadelgada/uploads/writer_ file/document/1121/tabela_de_taxas_e_licencas_2021_odt.pdf

Câmara Municipal de Sintra. (2018). *Regulamento e Tabela de Taxas e Outras Receitas do Município de Sintra para o ano de 2018.* https://cm-sintra.pt/ institucional/camara-municipal/taxas-do-municipio

Câmara Municipal do Funchal. (2019). *Tabela de Taxas e Outras Receitas Municipais 2020.* http://www.cm-funchal.pt/media/k2/attachments/ Tabela_de_Taxas_e_Outras_Receitas_Municipais_2020.pdf

Câmara Municipal do Porto. (2021). *Código Regulamentar do Município do Porto.* https://cmpexternos.cm-porto.pt/apex/f?p=150:1:0:::::

Câmara Municipal do Porto Moniz. (2010). *Regulamento de taxas compensacoes e tarifas do Municipio do Porto Moniz.* https://www.portomoniz.pt/ pt/documentos/category/128-taxas

Direção-Geral das Atividades Económicas. (2020, October). *Nota Informativa – Atividade Funerária – Novo Regime Jurídico do Funeral Social.* https:// www.dgae.gov.pt/servicos/comercio-servicos-e-restauracao/funeral-social-.aspx

Gabinete de Estratégia e Planeamento. (2021). *Boletim Estatístico Janeiro de 2021.* http://www.gep.mtsss.gov.pt/documents/10182/10925/bejan2021.pdf/ ead6e670-e1fd-4c4c-8e1a-b92047a39f7d

Junta de Freguesia de Esgueira. (2015). *Tabela de Taxas, Licenças e Emolumentos da Junta de Freguesia de Esgueira—2015.* https://www. jf-esgueira.pt/web/wp-content/uploads/2017/08/Taxas-Licencas-e-Emolamentos.pdf

Preços cobrados vão de 33 a 250 euros por cada cremação. (2008, August 9). *Jornal de Notícias.* https://www.jn.pt/nacional/precos-cobrados-vao-de-33-a-250-euros-por-cada-cremacao-976801.html

Queiroz, J. (2020, November 2). Perfume e música pedidos em vida para os funerais. *Jornal de Notícias*. https://www.jn.pt/nacional/perfume-e-musica-pedidos-em-vida-para-os-funerais-12988057.html

Tabela de Taxas e Tributos. (2008). https://www.diocese-porto.pt/media/1787/taxas_eclesiasticas.pdf

Xisto, B. O. de O. (2012). *"Assunto encerrado"? Atitudes contemporâneas perante a morte e a cremação em Lisboa* [Master Thesis in Social and Cultural Anthropology]. Universidade de Lisboa.

9 Burial

Current cemetery provision

There are no official surveys to indicate how many burial sites are currently operational in Portugal. Estimates in the press mention around 5,000 burial sites (Vieira, 2020).

These estimates include both public and private cemeteries, with public cemeteries in *freguesias* (civil parishes) making up the vast majority of the count. There are currently 3,092 *freguesias* in Portugal, and prior to 2013, when a territorial reorganization took place, there were 4,260. The majority of these *freguesias* had their own cemeteries, which remain active today.

There are also 308 *municípios* (towns and cities). Most *municípios* have their own cemetery, and it is common for larger *municípios* to have more than one. The city of Lisbon, for instance, manages seven municipal cemeteries.

Finally, private cemeteries round out the count, but their number does not exceed 30, nationwide. We can divide this group into Catholic cemeteries managed by religious brotherhoods (in Northern Portugal only, namely in Oporto); and British and Jewish cemeteries, which are located in some port cities in mainland Portugal and in the archipelagos of the Azores and Madeira.

Types of cemetery

The vast majority of cemeteries are established and managed, as stated, by the public sector. For this reason, the discussion in this chapter will be mostly focused on public cemeteries. Public cemeteries are managed, at the lowest level of government, by a *Junta de Freguesia* (civil parish council in charge of a *freguesia*) or, at the next higher level, by a *Câmara Municipal* (city hall in charge of a *município*).

DOI: 10.4324/9781003153689-9

Under the current legal framework, private entities may no longer establish cemeteries. They may only manage public cemeteries under a concession agreement or private cemeteries already in existence. For instance, Catholic brotherhoods in the city of Oporto established the cemeteries of Lapa and Bonfim in 1833 and 1849, respectively, and continue to manage them today. Protestant communities in Lisbon, Oporto, or Funchal retain the management of their own cemeteries, which date back to the 18th century.

There are no dedicated war cemeteries for Portuguese soldiers, but it is common for public cemeteries to include a *Talhão dos Combatentes* (literally, combatant's plot) not only for war casualties, but also for war veterans, both from World War I and the Portuguese Colonial War. There are, however, two very small war cemeteries built for foreign fighters: the oldest stands in the small city of Elvas and contains just five graves of British soldiers who were killed during the Peninsular War; the more recent, named Lajes War Cemetery, stands next to the military airfield of Lajes, in the Azorean island Terceira, having 49 graves, most with the remains of Royal Air Force members who died during World War II. There was also

Figure 9.1 The *Talhão de Combatentes* at the Conchada Cemetery, Coimbra.

another very small cemetery in the Azorean island of Santa Maria, near another airfield where USA troops operated during World War II, but this burial ground was dismantled when North Americans left the airfield.

Cemeteries and planning

City councils and civil parish councils are tasked with building, expanding, improving, and promoting the normal functioning of public cemeteries. According to Decree 44220, the choice of land for the installation of cemeteries or expansion of existing ones must be preceded by an inspection. This inspection should consider characteristics such as the size of the area, accessibilities, distance to residential areas, quality of the subsoil, among others. Once the location has been decided, city halls and civil parish councils submit a request to the government to receive approval from the entities in charge of territorial planning and health.

According to Decree 44220, the dimensions of a new cemetery must be calculated based on the number of inhabitants of the localities to be served (foreseen for the end of a period of 50 years) and on the average mortality in the last 5 years. No such guidelines exist for crematoria.

Cemetery layout

The general organization of Portuguese cemeteries follows Decree 44220, but there is some room for variation. By the time this Decree was published in 1962, almost all of the public cemeteries existing nowadays were already operational, in many cases following guidelines from the 1830s regarding construction and functioning. There is, then, a marked discrepancy between what national legislation establishes and what cemeteries are able to apply in reality. Modern cemeteries established in the 21st century may further this discrepancy by exploiting gray areas in national legislation.

According to Decree 44220, cemeteries should be as regularly shaped as possible (though what this means is not clarified) and bounded by walls, fences, or hedges between one and a half and two meters tall. The main entrance gate should be at least two and a half meters wide and feature, on the outside, a square with sufficient dimensions for the parking and maneuvering of vehicles, and for the movement of the funeral processions. Vehicles do not usually enter local cemeteries, but they may be allowed to enter large urban cemeteries, especially if the burial or entombment is taking place far from the main entrance.

Paths inside the cemetery are particularly well-regulated. There must be at least two paths, at least three meters wide and intersecting at the middle of the cemetery. Smaller paths must be at least two meters wide, and a narrower path, at least one meter wide, should follow the inner perimeter of the cemetery. Paths should be made of resistant materials: cobblestones and asphalt are both common, depending on the age and style of the cemetery. These particular guidelines are so ingrained that there is only one cemetery in Portugal with winding paths: the Cemetery of Agramonte, in Oporto, which was clearly inspired by the innovative landscape plan of the gardens of the city's *Palácio de Cristal*, inaugurated in 1865.

All cemeteries must be constructed to accommodate specific areas, such as temporary graves, perpetual graves, tombs, ossuaries, and green spaces. Decree 44220 states that green spaces should occupy no more than 30% of the area dedicated to graves. This regulation, combined with the practical need to make the most of the space available, results in a visual feature that is characteristic of Portuguese cemeteries, which is the almost total absence of greenery.

As they must accommodate multiple areas, cemeteries will often follow a zoning scheme: temporary graves occupy specific plots and perpetual graves others. Cemeteries that allow for different types of perpetual graves may separate them by plot as well: one plot may feature only in-ground graves, while another may feature vault-style graves, separated from one another both above and below ground. Family tombs may be built on their own plots, or on the edge of existing plots. Finally, communal tombs, aerobic decomposition modules (precast concrete compartments that promote the process of decomposition), ossuaries, and columbaria, because of their vertical structure, may occupy the edge of the cemetery, along the outside wall, or flank the paths inside the cemetery itself.

Though this is not mandated by law, sections dedicated to the burial of babies and children are also commonly created within cemeteries. Cemetery regulations may refer to these areas specifically as *sepulturas de anjinhos* or little angel's graves. In addition to their symbolic weight, which could justify this separation, these graves also present practical difficulties, since they are much smaller than regular graves and, therefore, do not fit inside the usual grid pattern.

All these regulations were published, as we have seen, in the 1960s, at a relatively late stage of cemetery development in Portugal. As such, there are plenty of cemeteries that do not follow these specifications. A typical example would be operational cemeteries which may be found, today, attached to a Catholic Church or—in the case of towns—enclosed by the walls of a former monastery, sometimes in the middle of a residential area.

Types of grave

It is difficult to present a definitive typology of graves one might find in Portuguese cemeteries, because different criteria will bring forth different nomenclatures. National legislation favors a temporal perspective. It uses the terms 'temporary grave' and 'perpetual grave' to distinguish between graves based on their concession type, but does not create further distinctions between, for instance, in-ground and vault-style graves. Similarly, it uses the term 'tomb' to refer to a variety of entombment options, which may be private or communal, underground or above-ground, and temporary or perpetual. In 1998, Decree-Law 411/98 introduced 'aerobic decomposition modules,' which share characteristics from both graves and tombs, creating further ambiguities.

Cemeteries have tried to circumvent this difficulty by creating more specific nomenclature based, for example, on the characteristics of each plot or on the type of construction of each grave. Although this facilitates the management of each cemetery, it makes comparison at a broader level difficult, because the nomenclatures do not coincide. We present some common typologies in Table 9.1. However, when discussing dimensions and technicalities borne from national legislation, we will follow the 'temporal' nomenclature.

Table 9.1 Most common grave and tomb types in Portugal

	Graves			Private tombs			
	Temporary grave	Perpetual grave	Perpetual grave with above-ground mausoleum	Flat tomb or tomb with small headstone	Tomb with above-ground mausoleum	Vault-chapel	Parietal tomb
Width	n/a		Equivalent to one to two graves	Generally, equivalent to two to three graves, may be larger			n/a
Includes burial vault/grave liner?	Generally, no	May or may not include a burial vault	Generally, yes				n/a
Includes underground crypt with shelves/ niches for coffins?	No		Generally, no; may have shelves or niches above ground	Generally, yes	Generally, yes; may also have shelves or niches above ground	Generally, yes; will also have shelves or niches above ground	n/a
Underground capacity	A single coffin	Generally, two coffins, stacked		With crypt: three to nine coffins, stored in one to two sets of shelves or niches; without crypt: six to nine coffins, stacked in groups of three.	Three to eight coffins, stored in one to two sets of shelves or niches.		n/a

Above-ground capacity	n/a	n/a	May have space for coffins and/or ossuary urns, depending on the style of mausoleum	n/a	May have space for coffins and/or ossuary urns, depending on the style of the mausoleum	Three to eight coffins, stored in —one to two sets of shelves or niches.	Three to five coffins stacked parallel to wall, or —six to ten coffins stacked transversely to wall
Type of coffin	Generally, wood	Wood or zinc		Generally, zinc			
Duration of concession	No concession. Grave may be occupied for three to five years and then for renewable periods of two years, until the body has decomposed	Perpetual					

Figure 9.2 The public cemetery of Funchal on Madeira island.

Note: This cemetery is one example of non-compliance with Decree 44220 regarding paths. The fact that perpetual graves have underground sections with entrances turned to the main path makes the path unusually large. At the same time, it makes it impossible to pave the margins of the path, since they have to be dug up to allow access to the underground sections.

Temporary and perpetual graves

According to Decree 44220, there are two types of graves: perpetual and temporary. Perpetual graves are those where a burial right has been purchased in perpetuity. Once the owner of the burial right dies, the burial right may be passed on to the heirs.

Figure 9.3 A flat tomb in the cemetery of Viana do Castelo from the late 19th century.

Note: It was supposed to be a vault-chapel, but plans were not completed. At the front, there is an entrance to the underground section.

The owner of a perpetual grave has the option to build a monument, which may be subject to cemetery regulations. Should they wish to build a monument, they will be fully responsible for its care and maintenance. They will not, however, be allowed to remove it or conduct any large-scale changes without permission. Should they lose the concession, the cemetery will take possession of the monument.

A perpetual burial right may expire for several reasons. For instance, certain cemeteries may consider that the concession is null if the owner does not build a monument within a certain time period. Historically, this rule was put in place to encourage early adopters of public cemeteries to embellish and, therefore, dignify the grounds with extravagant monuments. This rule may still be found in the internal regulations of some cemeteries today, but it does not specify whether the monument should be of a certain size or appearance—only that it should be built.

Over the long term, perpetual graves may also be considered abandoned if the identity or whereabouts of the owners are unknown and, cumulatively, the owners do not exercise their rights for a specific time-frame, usually of ten years. In such cases, the cemetery administration will publish an edict requesting that the owners present themselves

Figure 9.4 A typical vault-chapel from the late 19th century in Northern Portugal (Viana do Castelo), highly influenced by the sepulchral art of Oporto.

Note: Iron gates allow full visibility to the altar and to the shelves inside. Under the first shelves, there is extra space for urns containing exhumed skeletal remains. The upper shelves are closed with dark slate slabs. Epitaphs would be painted in white or carved in these slabs.

within 60 days. At the same time, the administration will post an 'abandoned' sign on the grave. If the owners fail to present themselves within the timeframe, the concession may expire and revert back to the cemetery.

Figure 9.5 Combined parietal and vaulted family tombs in the cemetery of Anha.

Note: This sort of tomb displays a certain Galician influence from the north of Spain, not far from this cemetery, which is located in the municipality of Viana do Castelo.

Temporary graves have no associated burial right. According to Decree-Law 411/98, these may be occupied for three years, after which the body will be exhumed (see below). Depending on the specific cemetery, monuments may or may not be allowed on temporary graves. The Lisbon municipal cemeteries have a series of preapproved models which may be purchased and installed on a temporary grave while it is occupied (Câmara Municipal de Lisboa, 2020). In other cemeteries, the style of commemoration may be restricted only to portable decorations, which can be easily removed.

Although this is not predicted on national legislation, most internal regulations require that bodies are buried along with materials that accelerate the decomposition of the corpse. These accelerators may feature different compositions depending on the brands that provide them, but they are generally composed of a variety of microorganisms and non-pathogenic enzymes. Ideally, they will be effective aerobically

Figure 9.6 A plot of temporary graves at the Alto de São João Cemetery, Lisbon.

Note: Some graves feature small preapproved monuments, while many others are left bare.

and anaerobically, so that they may be used in the widest variety of burial and entombment options.

Grave dimensions and technicalities

According to Decree 44220, graves should be grouped into plots (referred to as *talhões*) of up to 90 graves—or 300 in large cities, although the Decree does not define how large. For an adult, a grave should be, at minimum, two meters long, 65 centimeters wide, and 115 centimeters deep; for a child, one meter long, 55 centimeters wide, and 100 centimeters deep. Graves should be spaced at least 40 centimeters from one another, with at least 60 centimeters on one side. This guideline is often circumvented or downright ignored, especially in older cemeteries.

Generally, no more than two bodies may be buried on top of one another. The Decree does not state how much soil should separate the two coffins; it states only that the older coffin should be buried deep enough for the newer coffin to be buried at the minimum depth of 115 centimeters. Graves are generally dug by hand. Some cemeteries may also employ small mechanical excavators, provided that they have the financial resources and that it is possible to maneuver the machinery around existing monuments.

In cemeteries where burial space is still readily available, the majority of burials take place in in-ground graves, which are usually back-filled on the day of the funeral. From there, most families will wait a few months to a year before erecting a monument. The monument is then placed on the ground above the grave. Some providers may install the monument over precast concrete beams, so that the monument stays level even if the ground shifts. In cases where the grave includes a burial vault, which may be made out of stone, brick, or concrete in newer cemeteries, the monument will form the above-ground part of the structure. Into the 21st century, newer cemeteries in urban areas have started to lay out precast concrete vaults in advance, so that new burials may take place within individual 'cells' that do not require digging.

Legislation at the national level does not offer great detail on the dimensions allowed for grave monuments. Instead, this topic is generally

Figure 9.7 A new plot in the cemetery of Deocriste.

Note: This new plot in the cemetery of Deocriste (municipality of Viana do Castelo) displays three of the current trends in cemetery layout: minimalism, uniformity of headstones (which sometimes is hard to implement, since families prefer to choose according to individual taste), and the precast concrete beams in unused graves.

addressed in internal regulations, which may restrict the size and style of the monument and the materials that may be used.

Decree 44220 also defines the minimum dimensions for ossuaries. Unlike a charnel house, which stores the skeletal remains of multiple people, deposited or stacked, an ossuary stores the skeletal remains of an identified individual. Portuguese ossuaries are essentially niches

Figure 9.8 An ossuary wall at the Conchada Cemetery, Coimbra.

Note: Some niches are closed with traditional stone slabs, while others are closed with a glass pane.

built into walls. Each niche should be, according to Decree 44220, at least 80 centimeters long, 50 centimeters wide, and 40 centimeters tall. This size should be able to accommodate a box containing the skeletal remains of a single person. There should be no more than seven niches stacked above ground level, or on each floor, in the case of multilevel buildings built specifically for this purpose. Although the law does not explicitly state it, these guidelines are also followed, in many cemeteries, for the construction of columbaria—niches meant for the storage of cremation ashes in individual urns—as the space requirements are similar.

All the procedures associated with grave opening, closing, and general cleaning and maintenance are undertaken by cemetery staff. However, the construction, decoration, maintenance, and ornamentation of any monuments are the owner's responsibility. Owners that abstain from maintaining their concessions for a certain number of years may lose their burial right. Some owners may hire help to maintain and decorate the grave or delegate the task to an institution. It is possible to find instances where the deceased has named an institution as a beneficiary in their will, in exchange for a perpetual concession in a cemetery managed by the institution in question. In such cases, the institution will care for that person's grave; generally, the grave may even be marked with a sign or a tablet to that effect, in order to hold the institution responsible, in case of lack of maintenance.

Types of coffin

National legislation distinguishes between two types of coffins: wood coffins and zinc coffins. The latter are not fully made from zinc, but simply wood coffins outfitted with a zinc liner measuring at least 0.40 millimeters in thickness. Up until 1998, lead liners were also used.

The general rule is that temporary graves should only receive wood coffins, while perpetual graves may receive both wood and zinc. Cemeteries will create variations on this rule depending on the structural characteristics of the perpetual graves they offer; for instance, underground graves built in the style of a vault may only allow for zinc coffins. For entombment above ground, only zinc coffins are allowed, as they will prevent fluid leakage.

The correspondence between the material of the coffin and the type of grave is related to the process of decomposition. In temporary graves, which are meant to be reused, a wooden coffin should allow for quicker decomposition; in perpetual graves, where the concession is purchased in perpetuity, the speed of decomposition is not as important. National legislation does not mention whether bodies which have been subject to thanatopraxy are allowed in temporary graves, as this too could influence the speed of decomposition.

The process of accommodating a body inside a zinc coffin is more complex than inside a wood coffin. For the wake and the funeral, the body is placed inside the base of the zinc liner, which fits inside the base of the wood coffin. The presence of the zinc liner is not noticeable to mourners. It is only at the cemetery that the top half of the zinc liner is added, and the two are soldered together by cemetery staff. Finally, the lid of the wooden coffin is attached to the base, and the body can be entombed or buried. Because of these particularities, exhuming remains from zinc-lined coffins can be an involved process. We will examine this in the section dedicated to exhumations and grave reuse.

Visually, the coffins used in Portugal tend to be rectangular, with the same or similar width at the head, shoulders, and feet. The lid detaches fully from the base, and it may be flat or gently staggered, depending on the decorative style of the coffin. Because funeral homes are generally small and cannot keep multiple sizes in stock, the Portuguese approach to coffins is, in practice, 'one-size-fits-all.' Agencies will usually stock an average size that will fit adults of various statures. The coffin is then customized and outfitted with specific textiles, religious symbols, metallic handles, and other embellishments, at the request of the family of the deceased.

Exhumations and grave reuse

Exhumations and grave reuse are integral to the normal functioning of a Portuguese cemetery. In fact, both are time-honored practices that span centuries, as demonstrated by the existence of several ossuaries and bone chapels across the country.

The current process for exhumation and grave reuse has been written into law since 1835. Back then, bodies could not be exhumed before five years had passed since the burial. Today, Decree-Law 411/98 has shortened that period to three years, but many cemeteries, including the Lisbon municipal cemeteries, have verified that this is not enough for a body to fully decompose (Ferreira, 2016). Portuguese legislation predicts that, if a grave is opened and the body has not yet decomposed, the grave will have to be covered again and reopened two years later. In order to avoid this, many cemetery authorities are choosing to deviate from national legislation and retain the original five-year period.

It is relevant to note that the task of verifying whether a body has decomposed falls to the gravedigger, who may conduct only a visual check or test whether the bones are 'disconnected' from the soft tissue. In the latter case, the exhumation may be carried out.

Administrative exhumations, or those conducted by the cemetery in order to reuse burial space, make up the vast majority of Portuguese exhumations. They may occur at regular intervals, when temporary graves have expired, or whenever the need for burial space arises. In order to begin the process of exhumation, the cemetery administration will generally put up a notice and then contact the heirs directly in order to inform them of the upcoming exhumation.

Families are invited to attend the exhumation and define the destination to be given to the respective remains; they will also pay the associated exhumation fee. If families choose to have the skeletal remains moved to an ossuary, gravediggers will carry the skeletal remains to a specific area of the cemetery to be cleaned, disinfected, and dried. Throughout the process, the remains are accompanied by a metal plaque that identifies the grave they were lifted from. Once dried, the remains are transferred into an appropriate box, or ossuary urn, and placed in an ossuary paid for by the family. Ossuary urns can also be stored in private tombs. Some of these urns are artistically decorated and made to be seen, like the ones in faience in some cemeteries of the Azorean island of São Miguel. In some older cemeteries in Oporto, ossuary urns received epitaphs, and several were used to embellish the top of cemetery walls.

If families choose to have the skeletal remains cremated, the exhumation fee will also apply. From then, the process will develop as a regular cremation, and further costs may be incurred depending on the destination of the ashes.

If families do not express an interest in attending the exhumation, nor indicate the end to be given to the respective remains, the exhumation will still be carried out, but the skeletal remains will be considered abandoned. Three things may happen: the remains may be buried deeper inside the same grave, allowing for new burials but preserving the location of the remains; they may be moved to the charnel house; or, finally, they may be incinerated, and the ashes poured into a communal ash deposit. The last two options imply that the remains will not be traceable or retrievable should the families change their minds; Portuguese cemeteries tend to follow the first option, unless there is something that prevents it (e.g. it is not possible to dig any deeper).

Monuments are not usually an issue when temporary graves are cleared, since most cemeteries do not allow for their construction in the first place. The families may be asked, however, to remove any mementos left on the grave.

Administrative exhumations may also be ordered in order to clear perpetual graves and tombs which have been considered abandoned. In those cases, the skeletal remains will be considered abandoned. However, these exhumations pose a specific problem, as burial or entombment in perpetual graves and tombs may involve zinc or lead coffins. These coffins are particularly complex to exhume because national legislation states that, once sealed, these may only be opened under orders of the judiciary authority or for the purpose of incinerating the body and/or its skeletal remains. However, the law allows cemetery administrations to define under which conditions they will choose to open these coffins. Because metal coffins are built specifically to prevent fluid leakage, organic matter resulting from decomposition accumulates inside the coffin instead of seeping into the ground, as would happen in a wood coffin. As a result, the exhumation of a metal coffin poses a greater logistical challenge than the exhumation of a wood coffin, from which cemetery staff could simply retrieve dry skeletal remains. Health authorities will be called to provide an opinion and examine the state of decomposition of the body. Even if the coffin is opened and the remains are transferred, the cemetery administration is then tasked with disposing of the coffin, which poses another issue. Because of these questions, in practice, many cemetery administrations choose to avoid the process of opening zinc and lead coffins altogether. As far as we are aware, there is no discussion at the legislative level about the best way to manage this problem, or about a possible discontinuation of the use of this type of coffin.

Apart from these administrative exhumations, which are ordered by the cemetery administration, exhumations may also be requested by families (e.g. to move the remains to a different area of the cemetery, or to a different cemetery altogether). These exhumations are subject to the same timings as administrative exhumations, and may not be carried out before three years have passed since the burial.

Finally, judiciary exhumations are also possible: these must be ordered by judiciary authorities, such as the public prosecutor's office, and do not have to abide by any of the timings presented in this section.

Tombs

Tombs, both communal and private, are common in Portuguese cemeteries.

Communal tombs are buildings or structures made up of multiple compartments, each sized to fit one coffin. The burial right for each compartment may be purchased in perpetuity, or for a limited period, the exact duration of which will depend on internal regulations.

Decree 44220 defines that each compartment should be, at minimum, two meters long, 75 centimeters wide, and 55 centimeters tall. There should be no more than five compartments stacked above ground level or on each floor, in the case of multilevel buildings built specifically for this purpose. Compartments may also be built underground, provided that the rule of only five compartments per level is respected.

Figure 9.9 The communal tomb at the Agramonte Cemetery, Oporto.

Decree-Law 411/98 states that the appropriate type of coffin for entombment, whether in communal or private tombs, is the zinc coffin. The same document requires that these coffins are equipped with purifying filters and other devices necessary to prevent the buildup of decomposition gases.

Once the body has been entombed inside the compartment, the compartment is closed (but not necessarily sealed, since the coffin itself provides a seal around the body) with a stone slab, usually inscribed with the name and photo of the deceased. Recently, some cemeteries have come to install hinged doors on these compartments, so that families may easily open and close them on their own. Some cemeteries may also use frosted or clear glass doors, leaving the coffin visible. In these cases, families will often take great care to decorate the inside of the compartment.

Unlike communal tombs, which are built by the cemetery administration, private tombs are built by and for a specific individual or family. In order to build a private tomb, an individual may purchase a burial right in an area of the cemetery that is zoned for that purpose. Generally, the space allocated for a private tomb is equivalent to the width of two to three graves. Depending on the internal regulations, the individual may be able to build a monument for above-ground entombment, underground entombment, or a combination of the two. In most cases, the plans for the monument will have to be approved by the cemetery administration.

Private tombs vary greatly in external appearance, internal organization, and even capacity. Contemporary tombs often take on the appearance of small chapels, with shelves or compartments for coffins on one or both sides of the door. This style of monument may accommodate anywhere from three to eight coffins above ground; with an underground section, this capacity may be easily doubled.

National legislation does not regulate the matter of private tombs in great detail. It states only, in Decree 44220, that the space allocated for each coffin should be the same as in communal tombs. In practice, the technicalities of the construction and use of private tombs are dependent on the internal regulations of each cemetery.

Like perpetual graves, private tombs may be considered abandoned if the owners do not exercise their rights for a specific timeframe. In these cases, the cemetery will reclaim not only the space allocated for the tomb, but also the monument which has been built on it. The monument itself may be preserved (e.g. due to its architectural value) or sold at public auction. In the latter case, the new owners will purchase both the burial right and the monument, but may not be obliged to keep the monument if the administration does not consider it worthy of preservation.

Aerobic decomposition modules

Aerobic decomposition modules were introduced in 1998 through Decree-Law 411/98. Like cremation, they should have been regulated shortly after with a *Portaria* from the appropriate ministry, but none was published. To this day, aerobic decomposition modules remain unregulated.

Aerobic decomposition modules are essentially precast concrete compartments—which may be stacked or laid out side by side in the ground—that promote the process of decomposition. Unlike traditional graves, burial vaults, and tombs, aerobic decomposition modules are equipped with ventilation and drainage systems. Decomposition gases are expelled through air ducts (which feature filters to keep odors in and insects out) and fluids originating from decomposition are drained through the bottom of the compartment into a septic tank. There are claims that this technology may bring ecological advantages as well. The body is placed inside the compartment in a wooden coffin; because there is no dirt surrounding the coffin and air circulation is actively promoted, the process of decomposition should proceed as quickly as possible and preservation processes such as mummification and saponification should be kept at bay. Decomposition permitting, the body may be exhumed after three years.

In practice, aerobic decomposition modules are a new and improved form of temporary grave. They should promote high turnover while taking up less ground space, making them a practical solution to the issue of cemetery space. They may also present advantages in places where the soil itself does not have the right characteristics to promote decomposition. Some cemeteries, however, have installed these modules and are granting them as perpetual concessions.

Due to a lack of regulation, different companies will produce different types of modules for installation. Company Beiracruz, established in the town of Miranda do Corvo, has installed these modules in cemeteries all over the country, using both stackable modules and laid out modules. The company has financed academic and scientific research in order to better understand how decomposition works inside the modules, and how their design may be improved, since there is, at the moment, no legislation on the matter (Ferreira et al., 2017; Morgado, 2018).

Notable exceptions

We have explored burial in public and private cemeteries. However, there are some exceptions. Article 11° of Decree-Law 411/98 states that bodies may also be entombed in the national pantheon or in the private pantheon of the Patriarchs of Lisbon.

Other exceptions may be applied to people of certain categories, namely of a certain nationality or religious belief, who may be buried in specific cemeteries, as long as this is authorized by the respective city council. It is under this exception that we can integrate the old British and Jewish private cemeteries, which continue to function today.

A third exception falls on burial in private chapels, located outside the population centers and traditionally intended for the deposit of the corpse or bones of the relatives of the respective owners, when authorized by the respective city council. Essentially, this means that if families own chapels which have been historically or traditionally used for burial, they may continue to use them for that purpose, as long as they procure permission from the city council of the area. Historically, these requests have very rarely been granted, and this exception is not commonly translated into practice.

Over time, influential families have been able to create exceptions to the exceptions. For instance, at the Prazeres Cemetery in Lisbon, the Palmela family tomb, which is often considered to be one of the largest private tombs in Europe, is currently managed and maintained by the city council (partly due to its tourist relevance); however, it continues to function as a tomb for members of the family.

References

Câmara Municipal de Lisboa. (2020, November 17). *Sepultura—Revestimento.* https://informacoeservicos.lisboa.pt/servicos/detalhe/sepultura-revestimento

Ferreira, A. R. F. (2016). *Body disposal in Portugal: Current practices and potential adoption of alkaline hydrolysis and natural burial as sustainable alternatives* [Master Thesis in Forensic Medicine]. Instituto de Ciências Biomédicas Abel Salazar da Universidade do Porto.

Ferreira, M. T., Coelho, C., & Gama, I. (2017). Application of forensic anthropology to non-forensic issues: An experimental taphonomic approach to the study of human body decomposition in aerobic conditions. *Australian Journal of Forensic Sciences, 51*(2), 149–157.

Morgado, R. A. G. (2018). *Inumação em modelos de consumpção aeróbia: Estudo tafonómico das consequências da utilização de caixão e acelerador enzimático na decomposição* [Master Thesis in Human Evolution and Biology]. Faculdade de Ciências e Tecnologia da Universidade de Coimbra.

Nascimento, E., & Trabulo, M. (2008). *Cemitérios: Ordenamentos e questões jurídicas.* Almedina.

Vieira, H. (2020, March 27). Direto para o cemitério. Enterrem-se os mortos. Cuide-se dos vivos. *TSF Rádio Notícias.* https://www.tsf.pt/portugal/sociedade/direto-para-o-cemiterio-enterrem-se-os-mortos-cuidem-se-dos-vivos-11987735.html

10 Cremation

Current crematoria provision

The first crematorium in Portugal, at Alto de São João Cemetery in Lisbon, was reopened in 1985 after a long period of closure. Between 1985 and 1995, there were no other crematoria in the country; as a result, all cremations were conducted at Alto de São João. In the 1980s, foreigners made up the vast majority of cremations—as much as 61% in 1986 (Queiroz, 2005). By the 1990s, however, Portuguese nationals made up the majority. The second crematorium in Portugal was built in Oporto, 1995, at Prado do Repouso Cemetery. As in the case of Alto de São João, many of those initially cremated at Prado do Repouso were foreigners, specifically Hindu immigrants from India (Queiroz, 2005).

Between 1996 and 2000, no other crematoria were built. The turn of the millennium then brought a surge in crematorium construction. Nine new crematoria opened between 2000 and 2009, and 17 more from 2010 to 2019. In 2020 alone, six new crematoria were opened.

Both public and private crematoria exist in Portugal. Like public cemeteries, public crematoria are managed by local authorities; private crematoria may be managed by any private entity, as long as it meets the criteria of the legal regime of access and exercise of the funeral activity, explicit in Decree-Law 109/2010. In some cases, crematoria may also be built and managed under public–private partnerships. Suburban towns, where local authorities struggle with cemetery overcrowding but cannot afford to build a public crematorium, may benefit the most from these partnerships. As the private sector steps in and exploits the existing need for an alternative to burial, there is less pressure on local authorities to expand existing cemeteries (Xisto, 2012, p. 41).

DOI: 10.4324/9781003153689-10

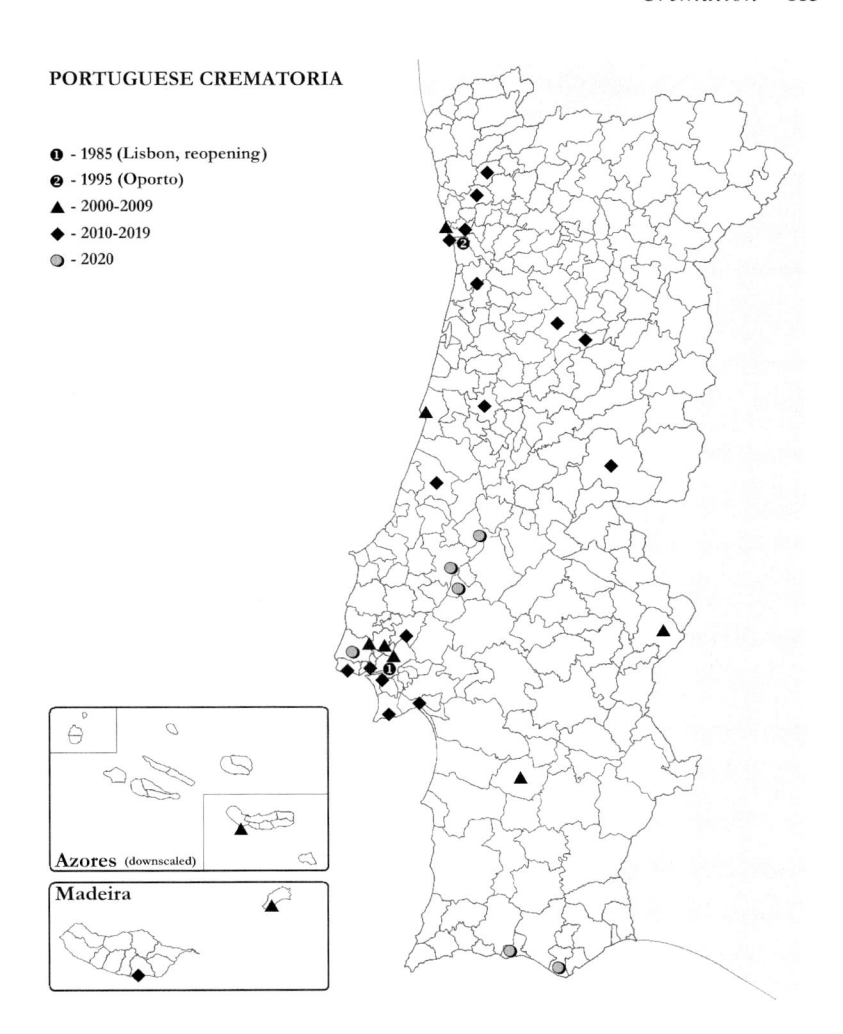

Figure 10.1 Map of Portuguese crematoria.

As of 2020, public crematoria make up the majority of crematoria in the country. Of the 12 crematoria managed by the private sector, eight belong to Servilusa.

Number of cremations performed in Portugal

No official statistics exist on the total number of cremations performed in Portugal each year. A 2015 survey reported 5,304 nationwide cremations in 2010, 7,696 in 2013, and 11,882 in 2014 (Gomes & Palma, 2015); however, there were significant gaps in the data, as multiple crematoria (including the five crematoria managed by Servilusa at the time) refused to take part in the survey. Crossing these numbers with the total number of deaths in the country for each year would result in a cremation rate of 5% in 2010, 7.22% in 2013, and 11.33% in 2014. Although incomplete, the data show that cremation rates are growing, which is consistent with recent numbers published in the press, which report that around 21,000 cremations were performed in 2019 (Salvador, 2020), equivalent to a cremation rate of 18.78%.

Cremation in Portugal remains mostly an urban phenomenon: in Lisbon and Oporto, the two largest cities in Portugal, cremation rates are over twice the national rate; in 2011, cremation accounted for 51.3% of all funerals in the city of Lisbon, and 47% of all funerals in the city of Oporto (Xisto, 2012, pp. 39, 41). This disparity may be explained, in part, by the timeline of crematorium construction, as well as the geographical distribution of Portuguese crematoria: Lisbon and Oporto had access to public crematoria before other regions, and to this day, a significant number of the existing crematoria are concentrated in these metropolitan areas. There are areas of the country, however, which are not served by any crematoria; for instance, someone living in Bragança, one of the most populous cities in Northeastern Portugal, will have to pay to transport the body over 100 kms in order to have it cremated, the cost of which may be prohibitive.

Crematoria design

Originally built in 1925, the crematorium at Alto de São João Cemetery was the only crematorium in the country for 70 years. As such, its architecture features unique characteristics that do not appear in any other Portuguese crematoria. The crematorium at Alto de São João occupies a prominent location in the cemetery, close to the main entrance. Although it is designed as a Neo-Romanesque chapel, the crematorium does not bear any explicit Christian symbols. Its purpose as a crematorium is clear: the chimney, which is integrated in the dome of the chapel, plays an integral part in the design (Oliveira, 2007); the sculpted entrance arch is decorated with skulls enveloped in flames. Beyond the arch, tile panels designed by Carlos Botelho depict cremation in ancient times. Originally, the building was fully open to the outdoors; a small art nouveau gate was the only thing separating 'inside' from 'outside' (Queiroz, 2005). A glassed-in

Figure 10.2 The crematorium at Alto de São João Cemetery, Lisbon.

vestibule was then added in the late 1980s, effectively adding square footage to the crematorium and increasing the number of people who could attend cremations. This updated design remains in use to this day.

The crematorium at Prado do Repouso Cemetery, in Oporto, marks the shift toward a more modern, utilitarian design. Designed in 1995 by architect Manuel da Silva Lessa, this crematorium renounces the chapel-like design and becomes decidedly secular in appearance. Its surroundings include an expansive lawn, featuring a contemporary sculptural work by Armando Alves (Queiroz, 2005), and a rose garden, which may be used for ash disposal. Unlike the crematorium at Alto de São João, the crematorium at Prado do Repouso is located at the far end of the cemetery. The placement of the crematorium in such a low-profile area was mainly the result of circumstances; that section of the cemetery was not in use at the time of construction, and so placing the crematorium there would not change the capacity of the cemetery. At the same time, it would dignify the space and the practice of cremation, as the area can only be reached through a tree-lined lane and, moreover, benefits from a panoramic view over the Douro river.

All other Portuguese crematoria were purpose-built in the 21st century. Like the previous examples, they are also non-denominational in appearance. Designed to provide a service that begins and ends within a few hours, their appearance effectively communicates this message: the buildings are simple and utilitarian, designed with minimal contemporary lines and stripped of any symbolism that may suggest an immediate association with death.

A crematorium may differ from a funerary center in terms of amenities. The simplest of crematoria may include as little as a covered entrance for mourners and a chapel or viewing room, as is the case with the crematorium at Alto de São João; the back portion of the building will then contain the cremator itself, as well as a separate entrance for employees. A funerary center, on the other hand, may include all sorts of amenities: a florist, a coffee shop, other commercial spaces selling funerary or religious items, ample parking space, indoor and outdoor gardens, an ecumenical chapel, one or more viewing rooms, and finally, a *sala de despedida* (farewell room) where close friends and family can say their final goodbyes to the deceased. Public crematoria are more likely to favor the former style, while private crematoria are more likely to favor the latter.

Like cemeteries, crematoria and funerary centers are free to define their opening hours in their internal regulations. Private crematoria may use a 24-hour schedule as a selling point.

The cremation process

As the corpse enters the cremation room, staff may check for any medical devices (i.e. pacemakers) or prosthetics which may need to be removed in order to ensure that the cremation process runs smoothly. Most crematoria remove pacemakers prior to cremation; some will also remove external prosthetics; few will remove internal prosthetics (Ferreira, 2016). Occasionally, this process will have been completed by the funeral director during the process of preparing the body. This may be beneficial, since it will remove an intermediate step between the ceremony and the cremation.

The family may be able to watch the moment the body is placed in the cremator; this will depend on the design of the crematorium; at Alto de São João, for example, this is not possible, since the cremator itself is located in a backroom where the family may not enter (Xisto, 2012). As mentioned earlier, cremation coffins should be made of wood and easily destroyed by the action of heat; in practice, they tend to be free from flammable varnishes and any excess ornaments.

Portuguese crematoria use a variety of cremators: a survey conducted in 2016, which obtained information from seven crematoria, found that four used two-chamber cremators, two used three-chamber cremators, and one used a one-chamber cremator. Maximum temperatures reported were between 700°C and 1200°C. All but two were powered by natural gas, with the exceptions being butane gas and propane gas (Ferreira, 2016). The cremation process may last as little as 75 minutes or as much as 180 minutes (Ferreira, 2016).

Once cremation is complete, any remaining bone fragments will be ground into a fine powder. There are a variety of processing methods that have been regularly used in the United States and Europe, such as hand-processing, ball/hammer mill processing, and a newer method called the rotary hinge blade processor. We do not know if one of these processes is favored over the others in Portugal. The resulting powder, which is generally referred to as cremation ashes, is then stored in a container; a numbered plate, which identifies the deceased and the family member who is responsible for the ashes, may be affixed to the container (Xisto, 2012). Finally, the ashes are stored or disposed of in the cemetery itself, or delivered to the family or to the funeral director.

Disposing of the ashes

As the first cemetery to include a crematorium, Alto de São João set the example in terms of the forms of ash disposal available in Portuguese cemeteries. The *Jardim da Saudade* (Garden of Longing) was the first area allocated to the burial of ashes; the ashes of each individual were buried separately in the garden, without the urn, and memorial plaques were not permitted. Later, the cemetery created collective cremation deposits, essentially large underground receptacles into which ashes could be poured (Xisto, 2012). Both options remain in use in the Lisbon municipal cemeteries.

The concept of a remembrance garden for ash disposal has also been adopted by other cemeteries throughout the country. Although naming conventions and guidelines for use of these spaces may vary, with some allowing burial and others allowing scattering, remembrance gardens or *roseirais* (rose gardens) have become commonplace.

A third form of ash disposal inside the cemetery involves placing the urn of ashes in a columbarium. A columbarium may be defined as a structure, either a building or a wall, with multiple niches into which cremation urns may be placed. Columbarium walls, similar to ossuary walls, are common in Portuguese cemeteries; each niche is covered with a metal or stone plaque which may be inscribed with the name of the deceased and decorated at will. Niches may be purchased, but they are most commonly rented for a set timeframe.

Decree-Law 411/98 states that ashes may also be placed in a grave, tomb, or ossuary; however, because these areas of the cemetery are not specifically designed for ash disposal, each cemetery will regulate how they may be used to fulfill this end, and the associated costs.

The ashes may also be delivered to those who have requested the cremation, usually the family of the deceased. They may be stored or scattered, either on land or at sea. The legality of scattering ashes at sea is often debated in the press. Nevertheless, multiple funeral homes offer this service, and the *Marinha Portuguesa* (Portuguese Navy) itself has stated that it will perform it if requested (Pereira, 2014).

In recent years, there has also been a rising trend in the commercialization of cremation-related products, such as biodegradable urns that, upon burial, turn into a tree, or memorial jewelry that incorporates the ashes.

References

Ferreira, A. R. F. (2016). *Body Disposal in Portugal: Current Practices and Potential Adoption of Alkaline Hydrolysis and Natural Burial as Sustainable Alternatives* [Master Thesis in Forensic Medicine]. Instituto de Ciências Biomédicas Abel Salazar da Universidade do Porto.

Gomes, J. M., & Palma, I. (2015, November 5). *A "moda" das cremações.* http://www.atesempre.pt/pt/content/16-noticia?id_noticia=5332#cat-5

Oliveira, M. M. (2007). *In memoriam, na cidade* [PhD Dissertation in Architecture]. Universidade do Minho.

Pereira, H. (2014, October 17). Quer deitar cinzas ao mar? A Marinha ajuda. *Observador.* https://observador.pt/2014/10/17/quer-deitar-cinzas-ao-mar-marinha-ajuda/

Queiroz, F. (2005). Portugal. In *Encyclopedia of Cremation.* Ashgate.

Salvador, J. M. (2020, June 13). O adeus ao corpo. Como a cremação está a conquistar os portugueses. *Expresso.* https://expresso.pt/sociedade/2020-06-13-O-adeus-ao-corpo.-Como-a-cremacao-esta-a-conquistar-os-portugueses/

Xisto, B. O. de O. (2012). *"Assunto encerrado"? Atitudes contemporâneas perante a morte e a cremação em Lisboa* [Master Thesis in Social and Cultural Anthropology]. Universidade de Lisboa.

11 Commemoration

Monumentation in churches and adros

Up until 1835, when the end of church burial was imposed and the concept of public cemetery was instituted, the way of commemorating the dead in Portuguese churches assumed somewhat different characteristics from what is found in other European countries. From the outset, the area around the church was characterized by a near-absence of monuments. We find the origin of this phenomenon in the structure of Portuguese society, which, during the Late Middle Ages and the Early Modern Age, was extremely hierarchical and divided between clergy, nobility, and commoners. The latter were the vast majority, and there were few bourgeois among them with the economic capacity to order funerary monuments. Thus, funerary monuments were almost only accessible to nobles, members of the clergy from noble families, and in cities, wealthy merchants. Since funerary monuments were intended to be as close as possible to the grave, or to the family crypt, and the most desirable locations were near the altars where priests said mass, this gave rise to three major types of funerary monuments in churches: parietal tombs, in the form of a sarcophagus or arcosolium (arched recess); private side-chapels, generally with a crypt underneath and a coat of arms above the altarpiece or arch, affirming the ownership of the chapel by a certain noble family; graves, which lay on the ground, generally rectangular in shape and with simple inscriptions, sometimes with only a short name and a date. These were common in many churches, even when other types of funerary monuments were not present.

As for the area surrounding the church—the *adro*—we have mentioned that it was not only used for burial, since it also served other functions. For this reason, it did not feature any funerary monument. In fact, the *adro* was considered undesirable by those who could afford funerary monuments, as it was too distant from the altars where masses were celebrated. Some exceptions, almost all from the Lower

DOI: 10.4324/9781003153689-11

Middle Ages, were the graves with discoid stelae at the head, which, being placed near the walls of the church, did not greatly hinder the commercial and meeting functions of the *adro*.

Monumentation in public cemeteries

The law of 1835 that conceptualized public cemeteries in Portugal intended not only to fulfil public health needs, but also to create spaces for the placement of funerary monuments for a new and growing urban elite. These were merchants, doctors, teachers, and other bourgeois who were less conservative and did not necessarily originate from noble families. This urban elite had money to order tombs whose size and type could not be accommodated within the churches. Besides, prior to 1835, the construction of more side-chapels in churches, with a view toward accommodating new tombs, was generally very expensive.

Figure 11.1 Scabiosa atropurpurea, or *Saudade*, a flower which is often carved in sepulchral monuments from the Romantic Era.

Note: A romanticist expression of loss, carved in one monument of the Prazeres Cemetery dating from the mid-19th century. The flower is *Scabiosa atropurpurea*. In Portuguese, it is popularly known as *Saudade*, a word that is said not to have a proper translation into other languages, but whose meaning is a sense of melancholy and longing for someone who is gone or far way.

From the beginning, monumentation in Portuguese public cemeteries was given its own space and, over time, it became almost a social obligation. Thus, it was during the period between 1840 and 1910 that many of the most grandiose tombs were built in Portugal. From 1910 onward, monumentation in cemeteries became more restrained.

The 20th century saw greater uniformity in monumentation, which is particularly visible in cemeteries or sections of cemeteries opened in the second half of the century. The placement of flat stones over graves and the use of inscriptions and photographs all became commonplace, while large tombs became rarer and less prominent in the overall Portuguese cemetery landscape. From the end of the 20th century onward, there was a tendency in Portugal to return to larger tombs, namely those in the shape of a chapel; however, we are not aware of any studies that explain this phenomenon.

Figure 11.2 The cemetery of Alhandra, attached to the church.

Note: Given the fact that the church of Alhandra stands at the top of a hill, isolated from the village houses, public health authorities in the 19th century tolerated the cemetery being right next to the church. In terms of landscaping, this is a typical village cemetery in the outskirts of Lisbon: in the older area of the cemetery, larger tombs (mainly in the shape of chapels) are displayed in rows along the paths, and temporary graves, or smaller perpetual graves, are relegated to the middle of the plots, hardly visible from the paths. The more recent area of the cemetery displays smaller memorials, corresponding to a time the investment in visual forms of remembrance was not as high.

Portuguese cemeteries are easily recognizable, as almost all are based on the models of cemeteries in Lisbon and Oporto (Queiroz, 2002). However, there are regional variations, which largely derive from two factors: the stone materials available in the region; and, to a lesser extent, the proximity to the Spanish border.

Up until the beginning of the 20th century, the Oporto cemeteries influenced mainly the north of mainland Portugal, while the Lisbon cemeteries influenced cemeteries across the country (mainland and islands). This was largely due to the desirability of materials available at each city: the local stone in Oporto was granite, which was hard and difficult to carve, while the local stone in Lisbon was *lioz*, a type of limestone similar to marble, which was light in color and much easier to carve. This led to *lioz* becoming a more desirable stone for gravestones, which resulted in it being exported from Lisbon to the whole country, including the archipelagos of Azores and Madeira. Because the transportation of the material was so expensive in the 19th century, a grave monument built from white *lioz* stone became an indicator of high social status in areas where *lioz* was not naturally available. Even in continental Portugal, the demand for this stone was such that

Figure 11.3 Spanish influence in the tombs in the town of Campo Maior.

Note: Spanish influence can be seen in these brickwork half-buried vaulted tombs in the town of Campo Maior, close to the Spanish border, contrasting with the vault-chapels in the background, made of marble slabs and in the style of the cemeteries of Lisbon.

some stonemasons from the Lisbon region found it profitable to settle in Oporto, just a few years after the first monuments were erected in the cemeteries of this city.

In some regions of the country with soft limestone quarries and a tradition of ornamental stonework, several distinctive tomb typologies emerged in the 19th century, with the municipal cemeteries of Aveiro, Coimbra, Figueira da Foz, and Leiria being examples of it (Queiroz, 2002). In these cemeteries, the influence of the funerary art of Lisbon and Oporto is barely noticeable in monuments built before the mid-20th century.

With the generalization of stone sawing machines and better means of transport in the 20th century, the Alentejo marbles, which until then had been used almost exclusively in that particular region, began to be used throughout the country. By the mid-20th century, the Alentejo marble had become dominant as the preferred stone in Portuguese cemeteries, and the use of *lioz* in new tombs became confined mainly to the region closest to its extraction area.

The materials are not the only difference between the Lisbon and Oporto cemeteries. In Lisbon, the first monuments in public cemeteries were profoundly influenced by the British Cemetery, which had been established a few years earlier. In fact, when stonemasons began creating tombs for the Prazeres and Alto de São João cemeteries, in the mid-1830s, they were essentially replicating the same style of simple tombstones they created for the Protestant communities of Lisbon. However, there was an appetite for tombs with greater pomp and splendor, and French-style tombs, particularly inspired by those from Père Lachaise, began to appear in Lisbon public cemeteries in the late 1830s.

While Lisbon's public cemeteries were influenced by British and later French typologies, in Oporto cemeteries, a new typology was emerging: the vault-chapel. This type—a monument in the form of a chapel—was first conceived in the Lapa Cemetery. The first vault-chapels were large constructions, built out of granite, designed to occupy the edge of the cemetery, so as to visually enclose it in the manner of the Italian '*campos santos*.' The central sections were left open for smaller monuments, thereby creating an inferred socio-spatial hierarchy. The way in which these first vault-chapels were laid out—all facing the central sections of the cemetery—led to the respective doors being wide, allowing a good view into the interior. Inside there would be multiple shelves, each housing a coffin that was not visible, as it was enclosed by a slab. This slab would then hold the epitaphs, which could be read from outside the tomb.

Figure 11.4 Headstones in the Prazeres Cemetery in Lisbon.

Note: Despite being influenced by the ones existing in the British Cemetery of the same city, these are placed in rows facing the path and not as headstones, revealing acculturation of a typical British typology.

Conversely, in Lisbon, the first chapel-shaped monuments exhibited different characteristics. They were smaller, and their positioning was also different: rather than distributed along the edge of the cemetery, vault-chapels in Lisbon cemeteries were placed along the paths of the cemetery, with the epitaphs on the facade, flanking the door. The door itself was small, just wide enough for the coffins to enter, and opaque—usually made from sheet metal, with only small openings for ventilation. These monuments were not designed to be peered into, unlike in Oporto, and so they were rarely ornamented on the inside.

Figure 11.5 Some of the oldest and largest vault-chapels at the edge of the
Lapa Cemetery, in Oporto, dating from the 1840s and the 1850s.

In terms of other tomb constructions such as arches, obelisks, columns, pedestals with statues, and rustic tombs, the difference between the cemeteries of Oporto and Lisbon is not so notable, although in Oporto it is more common to have iron railings enclosing the grave or tomb.

Contemporary grave monuments

The trends in monumentation in Portuguese cemeteries have changed throughout the years. There is greater design uniformity in the late 20th and 21st centuries, which reflects not only the mode in which monuments are acquired, but also greater regulation in the size of burial plots. By regulating the size of individual burial plots, cemeteries have also regulated the design of the monuments which may be built over them.

The discussion in this section pertains essentially to grave markers, as this is the type that most families will be purchasing today. The typical Portuguese grave marker is composed of two pieces: a horizontal

Figure 11.6 Partial view of the cemetery of Trancoso, which dates from the middle of the 19th century.

Note: Located outside this small town's medieval walls, in order to obtain a larger acceptance from the population, it was established in a former *adro*. In terms of landscape, this cemetery follows the pattern of the Lapa Cemetery, in Oporto, with the bigger monuments on the edges, defining part of the initial enclosure. The uneven terrain allows us to see the vaults under the family sepulchral chapels. The new area of the cemetery, from the late 20th century, has smaller monuments.

slab that covers the width and length of the grave, and a vertical headstone where information is inscribed. Some families may wish to forgo one or the other, but the vast majority of grave markers will follow this setup.

Grave monuments are sold by companies that specialize in the transformation and commercialization of marbles and granites. Although specialized companies do exist, most of the companies that sell grave monuments also sell other types of stonework.

The location of the premises of these companies can vary widely. In larger cities, the oldest stonework companies were often located either in the city center or near a wharf. Toward the end of the 19th century, new companies in big cities began to move nearer the cemeteries; then, from the second half of the 20th century onward, they moved out into peripheral areas, which were generally not far from the newer cemeteries. In less urban contexts, it is common to find stonework companies

Figure 11.7 A view of the Prazeres Cemetery, Lisbon.
Note: In the cemeteries of Lisbon, larger monuments are usually displayed in rows, along the paths, while smaller ones and temporary graves are hidden in the back of these rows.

Figure 11.8 Iron railings in the old cemetery of Vila Real.
Note: In the old cemetery of Vila Real, the influence of Oporto cemeteries is seen both in the typologies of tombs and in the intensive use of iron railings.

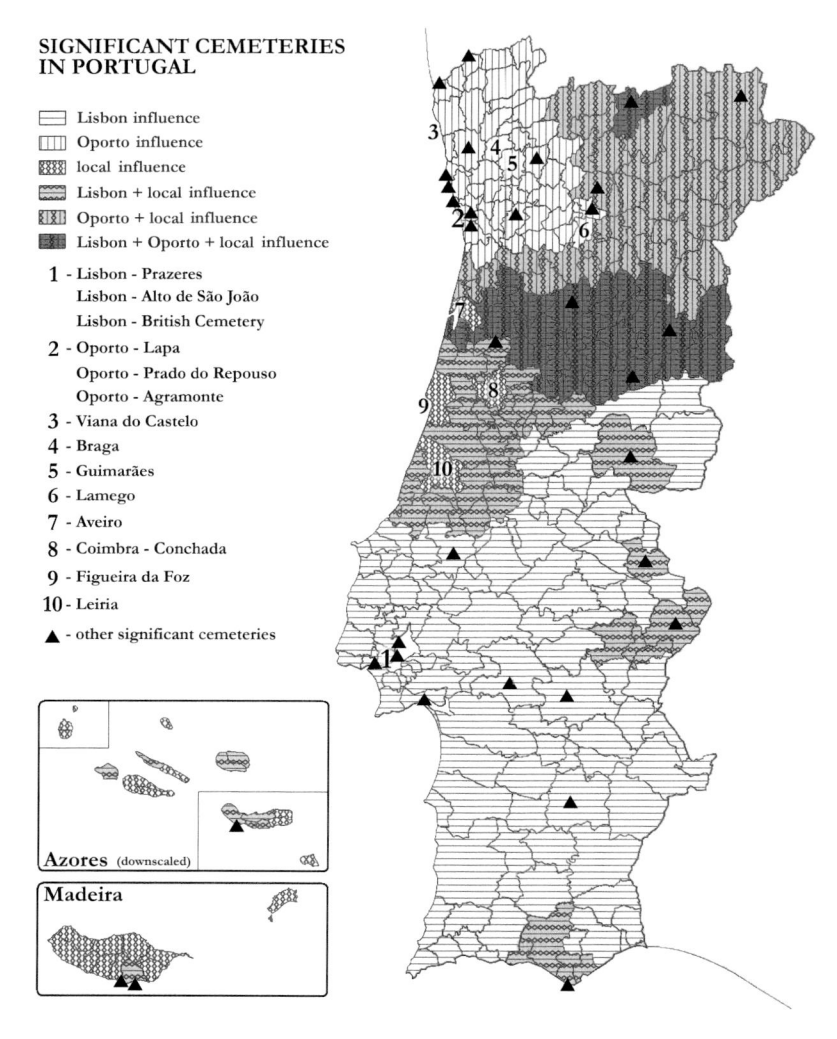

**SIGNIFICANT CEMETERIES
IN PORTUGAL**

☐ Lisbon influence
▥ Oporto influence
▨ local influence
▤ Lisbon + local influence
▦ Oporto + local influence
▩ Lisbon + Oporto + local influence

1 - Lisbon - Prazeres
     Lisbon - Alto de São João
     Lisbon - British Cemetery
2 - Oporto - Lapa
     Oporto - Prado do Repouso
     Oporto - Agramonte
3 - Viana do Castelo
4 - Braga
5 - Guimarães
6 - Lamego
7 - Aveiro
8 - Coimbra - Conchada
9 - Figueira da Foz
10- Leiria

▲ - other significant cemeteries

Azores (downscaled)

Madeira

Figure 11.9 Map representing the influence of Lisbon and Oporto in the most significant Portuguese cemeteries.

at a point on the main road between towns, or in industrial areas. When the time comes to select a grave monument, families may approach these companies directly by visiting their premises. Although many stonework companies have websites that include online catalogs of grave monuments, the pricing is very rarely on display; this means

Figure 11.10 Two tombs carved in local limestone from the 1880s in the cemetery of Conchada, Coimbra.

Note: This type of tomb, usually with a back entrance closed by a small opaque iron door, cannot be seen neither in the cemeteries of Lisbon nor the ones of Oporto, being typical from the Coimbra region.

that families often approach the company without any awareness of basic pricing information. The simplest of grave monuments may cost around 500 euros, with mid-range models falling around the 1,500 euros to 2,000 euros range. The larger and more custom the monument, the more expensive it will be; a tomb-chapel, for example, can cost as much as 20,000 euros.

At the stonework company, families may choose a grave monument based on display examples or peruse a catalog of available options. The company will source the materials, design the monument, manufacture it, and install it in the cemetery. Provided that the cemetery in question does not have any restrictions, families may choose everything from the type and color of the stone to the style of monument. While light marbles and grey granites are very common, one may also see pink, beige, or black stones. As for the design of the monument itself, the horizontal slab that makes up the lower part of the monument does not usually exhibit much stylistic variation, although its height is quite variable. Some slabs are practically flush with the ground, while others are almost knee-high. The headstone is far more variable in design. Some typical shapes for headstones include books, scrolls, hearts, angels, or wings. There are also simple rectangular headstones. Regardless of the format, headstones may also be decorated with other elements, which may be engraved or attached to the stone: crosses and crucifixes, floral motifs, angels, wings, or doves, and figures of saints (especially Saint Anthony or Our Lady of Fátima) are all common. Despite the availability of options, it is not often that a family will choose a truly custom monument. The result is that contemporary Portuguese cemeteries look very uniform, with little variation in the style of grave monuments. This is especially true in small towns, where there may only be one or two companies commercializing grave monuments from a catalog.

It is also at the stonework company that families select the information that will be placed on the headstone. The vast majority of Portuguese headstones include a photograph of the deceased. The headstone will also feature the name of the deceased, along with their birth and death dates. Epitaphs, if they exist at all, tend to be short and simple, such as '*saudade eterna*' (literally 'eternal longing'). This kind of epitaph can also be extended to identify the mourners: the epitaph of an elderly man may read, for instance, 'with eternal longing from his wife, children, and grandchildren.' All of the text placed on the headstone may be engraved or spelled out using metallic lettering.

Families that do not know where to begin the process of selecting a grave monument may also resort to a funeral home. While large companies such as Servilusa have the resources to sell grave monuments directly (Servilusa, n.d.), smaller funeral homes may only be able to act as an intermediary by recommending a stonework company. Another way families may select a stonework company is by looking through the monuments already present at the cemetery. It is a common contemporary practice for stonework companies to identify their grave monuments with a metallic label, which is usually mounted onto the monument at ground-level. This effectively works as a form of marketing, as families may find a monument that they like at the cemetery and easily contact the company in order to request a similar monument for themselves.

In regards to the timing of the purchase, some families will purchase the grave monument shortly after the funeral, while others will wait a few years. Indeed, it is not uncommon for graves to be uncovered for one to two years. It is possible, however, that cemeteries may restrict the amount of time a grave is allowed to be without a monument; this information, if relevant, will be present in the internal regulations.

Family visits and grave decoration

The traditional day for gravesite visits is November 1, All Saints' Day. According to Catholic custom, the appropriate day would be November 2, All Souls' Day, but the Portuguese have largely moved the practice to November 1, as All Saints' Day is a national holiday. Some families may just decorate their graves on this day, while others may do so regularly, either weekly or monthly, especially if the death was recent. In some rural areas, older women may take it upon themselves to visit every day. During cemetery visits, families will often clean the grave monument and leave flowers and candles for the deceased. Portuguese cemeteries have a number of objects available to help with the cleaning tasks: taps with running water, watering cans, brooms, and trash and recycling bins are often provided.

In regards to the objects that families leave at the grave, flowers and candles are the most common. Store-bought flower arrangements are usually only used at the time of the funeral; the rest of the time, families will bring homegrown flowers or bunches of store-bought flowers. They will then arrange the flowers at the graveside, on vases or planters that are placed on the horizontal section of the grave. It is also common for families to decorate with artificial flowers. As for candles, the candles used in Portuguese cemeteries are specific for the purpose, as they have a series of unique features. They are thick, usually white candles encased in a red or white plastic cylinder and topped with a perforated metal lid. This design makes the candle windproof, and therefore, more suitable for the outdoors. Cemetery candles may be bought not only at funeral homes and florists, but also at supermarkets and convenience stores. It is also common for graves to feature more traditional candles, usually inside glass or plastic lanterns. The use of battery-operated LED candles and even solar candles is also becoming more widespread.

Community-based commemoration

Two forms of community-based commemoration are relevant in Portugal: roadside memorials, which honor the victims of sudden or violent deaths (most commonly road accidents) on the site of their death, and *alminhas*, which honor the souls in Purgatory.

The construction of roadside memorials is widespread in many countries, with Portugal being no exception. Unlike a tombstone, which marks the place where a person's body is buried, roadside memorials mark the last place where the person was alive. At its simplest, a roadside memorial may take the appearance of a simple arrangement of flowers and candles; more elaborate compositions may include a memorial cross, usually made out of metal. Roadside memorials are usually located along national roads; they can be uncommon within residential areas, where the roads are not generally as dangerous, and they cannot be found at all on Portuguese highways, where they would be considered illegal.

Although most roadside memorials are created and maintained by family members or friends of the deceased, private and public entities may also create these markers for public figures, or for people whose deaths have struck a chord with the community. Due to their cultural and political bent, these memorials are more common within residential areas than the previous type. In the southern village of Baleizão, for instance, the community has erected a memorial to Catarina Eufémia, a member of the Portuguese Communist Party, who was killed by police during a protest in 1954.

Alminhas, another form of community-based commemoration, are particularly common in Northern Portugal. *Alminhas* (a term which may be translated literally as 'little souls') are small roadside shrines dedicated to the souls of the deceased—specifically, the souls in Purgatory. Authors place the beginning of their construction in the 17th century (Rodrigues, 2010, pp. 86). Located outside buildings, by the side of old paths and roads, *alminhas* are a common landmark in the Portuguese landscape—indeed, a village may be home to multiple *alminhas*.

Observably, *alminhas* are characterized by a panel that depicts the souls of the deceased, surrounded by the cleansing flames of Purgatory, using a variety of materials, from sculpted stone to painted tile (Lopes, 2016, pp. 223). The structure that surrounds the panel itself may present various appearances: it may take the shape of a small chapel, with a barred door through which offerings may be placed, or present simply as a niche in a wall. The panel, rather than its surroundings, is the defining characteristic of the *alminha*.

The underlying Catholic belief is that the souls of the dead may be freed from Purgatory and sent on to Heaven through prayer. Once there, they will display gratitude for the living they have left behind. In the end, the essential function of the *alminha* was to appeal to a form of prayer that should benefit both the dead and the living. Over the years, the practice has fallen into disuse, but it is possible to find communities where the *alminhas* are routinely cared for and decorated with flowers, candles, and even small offerings.

Online commemoration

The widespread use of technology and, in particular, social media has changed the way communities interact with news of a death. In the past, funeral directors would put up obituaries in public places where the community would know to look for them: on the doors of the church, on the windows of funeral homes, on shop windows, etc. These obituaries, usually printed on a sheet of A4 paper, would include the name and sometimes ages of the deceased, their photo, their area of residence, and all relevant information regarding the time of the funeral and the place of burial.

Today, these obituaries remain in use, but Facebook has come to play a vital role in the spreading of the same information. It is common for funeral homes to have their own Facebook page and to manage it in the style of a virtual bulletin board, where they post the same obituaries and provide the community with all the information they need should they wish to attend the respective funeral. The structure of the obituary has not changed, but the response that it elicits is new: now, the community can pay their respects directly on the Facebook page by commenting on the post. Family, friends, classmates, coworkers, and even just acquaintances are all able to mourn together, even if they cannot attend the funeral in person.

This model of online commemoration is fully employed on websites like *atesempre.com* and *infofunerais.pt*, websites with nationwide reach where funerary agencies, families, and friends can create tribute pages for the deceased. Families and friends are then invited to leave a message so they can preserve their memory of the deceased. Depending on the website, these messages may then be turned into a condolence book, which the family may acquire and preserve as a keepsake while the digital version remains online. Like the paper obituaries, the tribute page includes all the information one would need to pay their respects in person. Friends and family who cannot attend can also use the website to order flowers, which are then delivered to the family at the site of the funeral.

References

Lopes, M. I. A. (2015). *Alminhas: Image, Historical Time and Phenomenology.* The Fifth International Graduate Symposium of Art History Peking University, Peking.

Queiroz, F. (2002). *Os Cemitérios do Porto e a arte funerária oitocentista em Portugal: Consolidação da vivência romântica na perpetuação da memória* [Ph.D. Dissertation in Art History]. Faculdade de Letras da Universidade do Porto.

Rodrigues, O. M. de J. (2010). *As alminhas em Portugal e a devolução da memória. Estudo, recuperação e conservação* [Master Thesis in Art, Heritage, and Restoration Theory]. Faculdade de Letras da Universidade da Lisboa.

Servilusa. (n.d.). *Após Funeral.* https://www.servilusa.pt/pt/organizar-um-funeral/apos-funeral.

12 Conservation

Portuguese cemeteries founded in the 19th century or earlier, like those in other European countries founded in the same period, are exceptionally important repositories of various forms of art. In the Portuguese case, the architecture and sculpture found in cemeteries are sometimes associated with decorative arts in materials such as stone, metal, terracotta, faience, stucco, and stained glass, among others. Larger cemeteries, in the more populous cities that have experienced greater prosperity, are truly open-air museums—and even great archives, if we consider the enormous quantity of inscriptions, dates, and portraits they house.

Classification of cemetery heritage

The approach to cemeteries from the point of view of cultural heritage is a relatively recent phenomenon in Portugal. The awareness of Portuguese society on the subject has been a slow process, rooted both in the emergence of research on the subject and in the forms of public engagement, namely guided tours.

The first Portuguese studies that sought to draw attention to cemetery heritage emerged in the mid-1990s (Queiroz, 1997; Vieira, 1999; Sousa, 1994). At the time, only the Jewish Cemetery of Faro was listed as being of public interest (Direção Geral do Património Cultural, n.d.-a). Another cemetery, in the village of Maçãs de Dona Maria, was in the process of being listed as being of municipal interest.[1] The classification of cultural heritage determines that an asset has considerable cultural value, and that it should therefore be protected by law. There are three tiers of classification: heritage may be of national interest, public interest, or municipal interest. The classifications of national and public interest are awarded by the *Direção Geral do Património Cultural* (Directorate-General for Cultural Heritage).

DOI: 10.4324/9781003153689-12

The classification of municipal interest is awarded by municipalities, eventually with an opinion from the *Direção Geral do Património Cultural*.

In the city of Faro, the Jewish cemetery had been classified since 1978 (Iria, 1985). Despite its small size and the absence of monuments of great prominence, it was commonly featured in tourist guides. Interest in the Jewish cemetery in Faro is above all historical and limited to a specific community, in this case the Jewish community, which became extinct in the city; this, in turn, caused the cemetery to lose its function as a burial ground. Today, the Jewish cemetery is a place of memory, rather than a functional cemetery. The tahara house inside the cemetery, where the bodies were traditionally washed before burial, now serves as a small museum, along with a new wooden construction that serves as an interpretation center for the Jewish community of Faro in the 19th century. Elsewhere in the country, other Jewish cemeteries whose communities have practically disappeared are also in the process of being musealized: such is the case for the Jewish cemeteries in Angra do Heroísmo and Ponta Delgada.

As for the old cemetery in the village of Maçãs de Dona Maria, the reason that motivated the request for listing was its transfer to another location, far from the parish church. The process led to the partial destruction of the old cemetery, which made residents aware of the importance of preserving their past. Despite it being a cemetery of little prominence in the Portuguese context, the request for classification was seen as a possible solution to prevent the cemetery from being completely destroyed.

Both the Jewish Cemetery of Faro and the old cemetery in the village of Maçãs de Dona Maria were the object of heritage attention due to circumstances related to their local value. However, there are many cemeteries in Portugal with greater historical and artistic relevance. After a preinventory fieldwork carried out in almost the entire Portuguese territory (Queiroz, 2002), some Portuguese cemeteries were proposed for classification in 2002–2003, based on objective criteria of historical–artistic value.

National interest

The following cemeteries were proposed for classification as being of national interest:

- The British Cemetery of Lisbon, which is the oldest cemetery in Portugal, with more than 300 years of continuous use;

- The Lapa Cemetery, which is the oldest private Catholic cemetery in Portugal and the most influential cemetery in Oporto, having served as inspiration for many other cemeteries in the north of the country;
- The Prazeres Cemetery, which is the most ostentatious cemetery in Lisbon.

However, as of 2021, no cemeteries have been classified as being of national interest (from this list or otherwise).

Public interest

Given the artistic quality, originality, or quantity of monuments, among other factors, additional cemeteries were also proposed for classification as being of public interest:

- The Cemetery of Viana do Castelo;
- The Cemetery of Braga;
- The Cemetery of Guimarães;
- The Agramonte Cemetery, in Oporto;
- The Prado do Repouso Cemetery, in Oporto;
- The Cemetery of Lamego;
- The Central Cemetery of Aveiro;
- The Conchada Cemetery, in Coimbra;
- The Old Cemetery of Figueira da Foz;
- The Santo António do Carrascal Cemetery, in Leiria;
- The Alto de São João Cemetery, in Lisbon.

As of 2021, none of the proposals have moved forward, and no cemeteries besides the old Jewish Cemetery of Faro, which we have discussed, have been classified, on their own, as being of public interest.

However, some cemeteries have been classified as being of public interest because they are adjacent to another building that has been classified as such; in these cases, the cemetery is listed as being part of a group or cluster of monuments. The chief example among these is the Lapa Cemetery in Oporto, which has been listed as being of public interest along with the Lapa Church (Direção-Geral do Património Cultural, 2013). The official listing places greater emphasis on the church and does not feature any photos of the cemetery beyond the entrance gate. The information pertaining to the relevance of the cemetery focuses on its antiquity (as this is the oldest 'modern' cemetery in Portugal), its status as a burial ground for the local Oporto elite throughout the 19th century, the originality of its layout (we explore this in Chapter 11), and its influence on other cemeteries throughout the country.

Other examples of cemeteries that have been listed as part of a cluster of monuments include a cemetery in Arraiolos, the Meijinhos Cemetery in Lamego, and a cemetery in Vila Chã da Braciosa. None of the listings make mention of why the cemetery, in particular, is considered of cultural interest (Direção-Geral do Património Cultural, n.d.-b–n.d.-d).

Municipal interest

The cemetery in the village of Maçãs de Dona Maria has been classified as being of municipal interest since 1997, but does not appear as listed on the *Direção Geral do Património Cultural* (Directorate-General for Cultural Heritage) website. Beyond it, there are no other cemeteries classified as being of municipal interest, whether on their own or along with a nearby building. In Lisbon, however, there is a mausoleum classified as being of municipal interest: the Mausoleum of the Viscount of Valmor at the Alto de São João Cemetery.

A note on the classification of funerary heritage

The general conclusion is that there are very few, indeed very few, classified cemeteries in Portugal, the majority of which were classified because they were next to a classified building. When it comes to cemeteries being listed on their own, no cemeteries have been classified as being of national interest, only one has been classified as being of public interest (the Jewish Cemetery of Faro), and only one has been classified as being of municipal interest (the cemetery in the village of Maçãs de Dona Maria).

These two examples were listed because the cemeteries were no longer in current use, and the classification served to prevent them from being abandoned or dismantled. However, because the cemetery in the village of Maçãs de Dona Maria does not appear as listed on every government website, this leaves the old Jewish cemetery in Faro as the only officially listed cemetery in Portugal.

Cultural activities

The historical and artistic value of several Portuguese cemeteries has come to be recognized in other ways in recent years—for instance, through guided tours.

Figure 12.1 One of the first attempts to musealize a particular tomb at the Prazeres Cemetery, Lisbon.

Lisbon takes the lead in the organization of guided cemetery tours, especially in the case of the Prazeres Cemetery, as it was the first cemetery in Portugal to receive regular guided tours, from the mid-1990s. It was also the first cemetery to present several organized routes, with their own signage, and the first to include a visitable place with objects collected from abandoned tombs. Finally, from the end of the second decade of the 21st century, it was the first cemetery to offer guided tours in a language other than Portuguese, aimed specifically at tourists. Of all the Portuguese cemeteries still in use, the Prazeres Cemetery also stands out for having more tourist visitors than mourners, on a daily basis. It is one of the most important cemeteries in Europe, due to the scale, interest, and variety of its monuments. The Alto de São João Cemetery, in Lisbon, has received guided tours in recent years, since it is also a monumental cemetery, although less opulent than the Prazeres Cemetery. The British Cemetery of Lisbon is also regularly frequented by tourists.

In Oporto, guided tours of cemeteries began in 1999, at the Lapa Cemetery. At the beginning of the 21st century, tours began to be made

Figure 12.2 Tourists at the Prazeres Cemetery in Lisbon.

in the municipal cemeteries of Prado do Repouso and Agramonte as well, and with increasing regularity.

Guided tours were also held in some smaller cemeteries on the outskirts of Lisbon and Oporto (Loures and Sacavém, in the case of Lisbon; Paranhos, Matosinhos, and Leça do Balio, in the case of Oporto). In all these cases, the visits were mainly aimed at the Portuguese public, addressing historical and artistic themes. Guided tours held in other cities, such as Ponta Delgada, Viana do Castelo, Braga, Coimbra (Conchada cemetery), or Leiria, followed the same pattern, in that they are generally organized with a Portuguese audience in mind.

In addition to guided tours (some of which have been held at night), Portuguese cemeteries have also served as a setting for other types of activities and events in recent years: concerts (several of them held next to the graves of composers or musicians), dramatized tours, exhibitions, and even photography scavenger hunts. The Oporto city hall has been organizing, annually since 2005, the *Ciclo Cultural dos Cemitérios Municipais do Porto (Cultural Cycle of Oporto Municipal Cemeteries)*, a set of guided tours and other cultural activities that explore the potential of the city's cemeteries. Although it is difficult to obtain accurate statistics, every year the number of guided tours and other events in Portuguese cemeteries has grown, as has the number of participants (with the exception of 2020–2021, due to the COVID-19 pandemic).

Despite all this, threats to the conservation of Portuguese cemetery heritage are many and persist in almost all cemeteries, since few have changed their internal regulations or adopted specific measures to safeguard and protect their historical and artistic value. The main threat is related to the abandonment of perpetual concessions, and the consequent process of re-concession. On one hand, abandonment may cause irreparable losses in artistic terms. On the other hand, a new concession, even if it provides for the restoration of the monument, may entail the loss of historical information such as portraits and inscriptions.

Other sites of 'dark tourism'

Other sites in Portugal that are not strictly cemeteries have attracted tourist attention in recent years—they can be considered to be a part of, if not cemetery tourism, at least dark tourism (Coutinho, 2012). This is the case of some 'bone chapels' located in the south of mainland Portugal, which date from the 17th and 18th centuries, the best known being those in Évora and Campo Maior. It is also the case of the catacombs of the Irmandade de São Francisco museum, in Oporto, which date from the 18th and 19th centuries.

Note

1 According to *monumentos.gov.pt*, an official government database that documents the Portuguese architectural, urban, and landscape heritage, the cemetery of Maçãs de Dona Maria remains in the process of being listed as being of municipal interest since 1997 (Direção-Geral do Património Cultural, 2011). However, the cemetery does not appear on *patrimoniocultural.gov.pt*, another official government database that lists heritage sites which are listed or in the process of being listed. Both sites are run by the *Direção Geral do Património Cultural* (Directorate-General for Cultural Heritage). The incongruity between the two databases reflects the difficulty of offering a complete and updated picture of what is classified cemetery heritage in Portugal.

References

Coutinho, B. (2012). *Há morte nas catacumbas?: Um estudo sobre turismo negro* [Master Thesis in Tourism Management and Planning]. Universidade de Aveiro.

Direção-Geral do Património Cultural. (n.d.-a). *Antigo cemitério da colónia judaica de Faro*. http://www.patrimoniocultural.gov.pt/pt/patrimonio/patrimonio-imovel/pesquisa-do-patrimonio/classificado-ou-em-vias-de-classificacao/geral/view/74875

Direção-Geral do Património Cultural. (n.d.-b). *Convento de São Francisco e cemitério anexo*. http://www.patrimoniocultural.gov.pt/pt/patrimonio/patrimonio-imovel/pesquisa-do-patrimonio/classificado-ou-em-vias-de-classificacao/geral/view/73658

Direção-Geral do Património Cultural. (n.d.-c). *Igreja de São Cristóvão, paroquial de Vila Chã da Braciosa, incluindo o cemitério*. http://www.patrimoniocultural.gov.pt/pt/patrimonio/patrimonio-imovel/pesquisa-do-patrimonio/classificado-ou-em-vias-de-classificacao/geral/view/341952

Direção-Geral do Património Cultural. (n.d.-d). *Igreja paroquial, adro e cemitério de Meijinhos*. http://www.patrimoniocultural.gov.pt/pt/patrimonio/patrimonio-imovel/pesquisa-do-patrimonio/classificado-ou-em-vias-de-classificacao/geral/view/156248

Direção-Geral do Património Cultural. (2011). *Cemitério de Maçãs de Dona Maria*. http://www.monumentos.gov.pt/Site/APP_PagesUser/SIPA.aspx?id=3315

Direção-Geral do Património Cultural. (2013). *Igreja e Cemitério de Nossa Senhora da Lapa*. http://www.patrimoniocultural.gov.pt/pt/patrimonio/patrimonio-imovel/pesquisa-do-patrimonio/classificado-ou-em-vias-de-classificacao/geral/view/5975244

Iria, A. (1985). Os Judeus no Algarve Medieval e o Cemitério Israelita de Faro do século XIX. História e epigrafia. *Anais Do Município de Faro, 14*.

Queiroz, F. (1997). *O ferro na arte funerária do Porto oitocentista. O Cemitério da Irmandade de Nossa Senhora da Lapa, 1833–1900* [Master Thesis in Art History]. Faculdade de Letras do Porto.

Sousa, G. de V. e. (1994). *Cemitérios Portuenses: História e arte* [Final degree project in Historical Sciences]. Universidade Portucalense.

Vieira, P. C. A. dos R. P. (1999). *Os cemitérios de Lisboa no século XIX. Pensar e construir o novo palco da memória* [Master Thesis in Art History]. Faculdade de Ciências Sociais e Humanas da Universidade Nova de Lisboa.

Index